W9-BNN-299

VIETNAM

An Illustrated History

ILLUSTRATED HISTORIES FROM HIPPOCRENE

Published...

Arizona
Patrick Lavin

Celtic World
Patrick Lavin

China
Yong Ho

Cracow
Zdzislaw Zygulski

England
Henry Weisser

France
Lisa Neal

Greece
Tom Stone

Ireland
Henry Weisser

Israel
David C. Gross

Italy
Joseph F. Privitera

Korea
David Rees

Mexico
Michael Burke

Paris
Elaine Mokhtefi

Poland
Iwo Cyprian Pogonowski

Poland in World War II
Andrew Hempel

Russia
Joel Carmichael

Spain
Fred James Hill

Tikal
John Montgomery

Vietnam
Shelton Woods

Forthcoming...

Egypt
Fred James Hill

Gypsy World
Atanas Slavov

London
Nick Awde & Robert Chester

Moscow
Kathy Murrell

Portugal
Lisa Neal

Romania
Nicholas Klepper

Sicily
Joseph F. Privitera

Venice
Lisa Neal

Wales
Henry Weisser

VIETNAM

AN ILLUSTRATED HISTORY

SHELTON WOODS

HIPPOCRENE BOOKS, INC.
New York

Copyright 2002 Shelton Woods

ISBN 0–7818–0910–X

For information, address:
HIPPOCRENE BOOKS, INC.
171 Madison Avenue
New York, NY 10016
www.hippocrenebooks.com

Cataloging–in–Publication data available from the Library of Congress.

Printed in the United States of America.

To Lindsay

ACKNOWLEDGEMENTS

There are many people who helped to produce this book. I appreciate Daryl Jones and the Maddy family for allowing me to use pictures from their collections. The Vietnam Club at Boise State University did some translating work for this volume and I wish to thank them. Gwen Pittam of Boise State's Albertson's Library is the best friend a professor can have. Her tireless work to retrieve volumes from around the world is much appreciated. Guen Johnson in our History Department always goes beyond the call of duty. Paul Simpson at Hippocrene Books was supportive from the beginning to the completion of this project. Thank you for your editorial suggestions. Raymona Maddy critiqued the entire manuscript. Thank you for your thoughtful comments. Finally, I'm deeply appreciative for the assistance provided by Karen, my wife. Thank you for your critiques, encouragement, and help with the maps.

CONTENTS

INTRODUCTION

Tragic and heroic—these two words capture the essence of Vietnam. These terms are consciously placed in sequence because no matter what difficulties Vietnam faces, there is a triumph in its people that transcends immediate troubles. Vietnamese, a people historically dominated at various periods by empire nations including China, Japan, France, and the United States, have never lost their identity. That alone is a remarkable feat and a testament to the rich and deep culture that pervades Vietnamese society. This brief study is a tribute to the resilience of the Vietnamese people. The story of Vietnam begins more than two thousand years ago. Readers might be more familiar with Vietnam's recent history, including its wars with France, the United States, and China. This study is insufficient to cover the multifaceted aspects that encompass Vietnam, but it is hoped that it will be a doorway that many walk through to find a much broader vista to gaze upon and study.

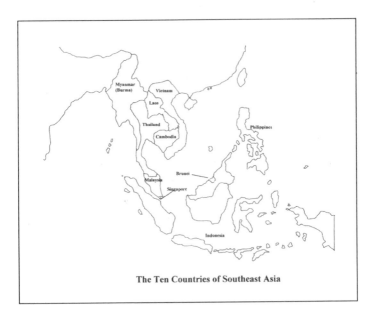

The Ten Countries of Southeast Asia

VIETNAM'S GEOGRAPHY

In one of his ballads, James Taylor, the well-known American folksinger, describes the planet earth as a "little blue ball falling around the Sun; one in a million billion twinkling lights shining out for no one." Indeed, one result of modern science is a fuller appreciation of the universe's size, and how our planet is a mere speck in relation to the vastness of the cosmos. Yet even on the earth's surface, the geographical position of islands and continents has shaped the history of nations and states. This is particularly true of Vietnam, whose physical location has influenced its history, society, religion, and economy. It is proper, then, to begin a study of Vietnam's history with an eye on its land and its place on this terrestrial blue sphere.

Vietnam is one of the ten countries that compose Southeast Asia, the others being Myanmar, Thailand, Cambodia, Laos, Malaysia, Singapore, Philippines, Indonesia, and Brunei. Coined during World War II, "Southeast Asia" is a relatively new designation for the lands between India and China. Formerly, this region was referred to as Greater India, Greater China, or Indochina—terms that reflect the influence of these civilizations on the development of ancient Southeast Asian states, particularly Vietnam.

Northern Vietnam borders China, a proximity that has facilitated steady economic, religious, and political interactions between these states. At the same time, Vietnam enjoys more than 3,250 kilometers of coastline and ports that have been the

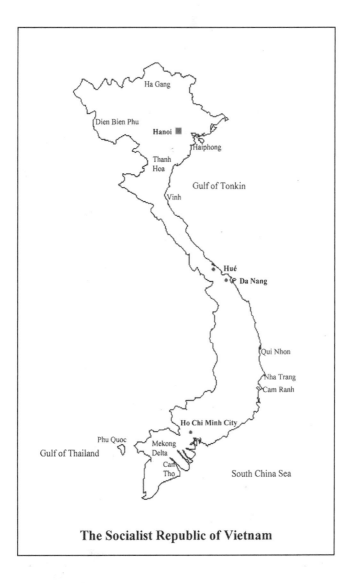

The Socialist Republic of Vietnam

perfect venue to trade with China. Thus Vietnam benefited from a cosmopolitan atmosphere early on in its history, hosting Chinese merchants and missionaries, and traders from India and other major kingdoms in Southeast Asia.

Today the length of Vietnam is 1,650 kilometers, stretching from China's southern coast to the Gulf of Thailand. The total area of the country covers 329,000 square kilometers, approximately the size of the U.S. state of New Mexico. Despite this relatively limited size, Vietnam is the world's thirteenth most populous nation, with eighty million citizens. Its climate is tropical with a rainy season (May to October), and a dry season (November to April). The average humidity in Vietnam is eighty-four percent and some portions of the country receive more than 300 centimeters of rainfall annually.

Shaped like an "S," the country is divided into three regions: North, Central, and South Vietnam. With Hanoi as its urban center, northern Vietnam developed more rapidly than other sections of the country. The fertile soil along the Red River allowed an agrarian-based society to develop and prosper in northern Vietnam.

During the nineteenth century, Emperor Gia Long unified all of Vietnam. He chose to build his palace in Hue, which is in central Vietnam. In portions of this middle region, the width between the sea and Vietnam's western neighbor, Laos, is less than fifty kilometers. The limited land area in central Vietnam means that many of its inhabitants find their primary means of employment in sea-related activities.

Southern Vietnam corresponds to America's "Wild West." Even in the early 1900s, South Vietnam was perceived as a frontier area. It was the region of Vietnam's former enemies and was underdeveloped compared to the rest of the country. Western imperialists were attracted to southern Vietnam because of the Mekong Delta's potentially rich agricultural lands. Today the farms along the Mekong River have made Vietnam the world's third leading exporter of rice. This southern plain of Vietnam is important for the country's agricultural output.

Vietnam's control of its southern neighbors was a slow process that ended only in the fifteenth century A.D., at which point a steady trickle of Vietnamese farmers moved into this frontier. However, despite the rich soil around the Mekong River, southern Vietnam remained sparsely populated until the twentieth century. One reason that there was not a major migration south is that Vietnam's social structure is centered on the village. In the past, one's identity in Vietnam was connected to his or her local village. Sacred burial grounds were in close proximity to the village, and acts of devotion included maintaining these areas. Thus the move south meant that northerners had to abandon villages that had been part of the family's history for generations. Moreover, the land that awaited them was usually nothing more than a mosquito-infested swamp that needed to be drained and deforested.

There were also remnants of older empires in the South, and ethnic tension characterized the social interaction between the area's indigenous population and Vietnamese migrants. Saigon eventually became the urban center in the South and remains so today, though its name has been changed to Ho Chi Minh City.

We will see that the French tried to use the three regions of Vietnam to create separate states. One unintended consequence of imperialist attempts to divide Vietnam was the growth of nationalism, which culminated in 1975 with the unified state that

The Mekong River.

Mountains on the road to Sa Pa, near the Vietnam-China border. Only twenty percent of Vietnam's land is level, with the remaining area covered by mountains.

we now call the Socialist Republic of Vietnam. The following pages tell the story of a journey that has lasted more than 2,000 years—a journey that includes numerous triumphs, tragedies, and the ultimate victory of the Vietnamese people.

Vietnam Before
Chinese Domination

Lac Long Quan

While we do not have verifiable figures in Vietnam's history until 250 B.C., folklore points to a mythical figure name Lac Long Quan as the father of the Vietnamese people. According to one variant of the Lac Long Quan myth, this Dragon Lord came out of the sea and subdued the demons in the Red River Delta. He instructed the people to cultivate rice and build irrigation canals to create a more sophisticated civilization. He then returned to the sea with the promise that he would revisit them should they ever need his assistance. As the legend goes, the people did need the aid of Lac Long Quan when a northern king sought to rule over the Red River Delta. The Dragon Lord dutifully returned and defeated the northern king. He also captured the king's wife (Au Co), and together they had 100 sons. One of these sons established the Hung dynasty, which lasted until the third century B.C.

While there are obvious apocryphal overtones in this myth, there are three themes in it that are instructive. First, it is clear that from the earliest days the Vietnamese were concerned about their powerful northern neighbor. Second, the idea of a god from the waters that exacts vengeance mirrors the existence of powerful typhoons that bring annual flooding and disaster to

Vietnam. Finally, there are records of a military buccaneer who entered the region in the third century B.C. and united the peoples in the delta area (the Lac Viet) with the peoples who lived on the periphery of the valley (the Au Viet) to create the state of Au Lac. Since Au Lac is an early name for the state in northern Vietnam, we can conclude that the early Vietnamese folktales are a mixture of myth and historical reality.

There is archaeological evidence that an early Bronze-Age society developed along the Red River beginning in the third millennium B.C. Artifacts from this period include arrowheads, spearheads, knives, fishhooks, and axes. During the transition period from the use of bronze to iron, a proliferation of drums were manufactured in this region. Decorated with pictures of birds, deer, and warriors, these drums were symbols of status and used in religious ceremonies. Early metaphysical beliefs mirrored the ideas of Vietnam's more culturally sophisticated northern neighbor, China.

Heaven, Earth, and Humanity

Unlike other major civilizations, China and Vietnam do not have creation stories. Rather, there is an understanding that the universe is divided into three portions: heaven, earth, and the realm between these two places. Early in its civilization, China ascribed the guiding force of the universe to a somewhat impersonal, all-powerful deity who was known as Shang-ti, or "Lord on High." As time passed, the pantheon of gods in both the Chinese and Vietnamese worlds included deities related to war, weather, and agriculture. To the Vietnamese, it was clear that while heaven existed on a different plain of reality, it was imperative to keep harmony between heaven and earth. Among other things, cosmic harmony was maintained by revering one's father. Veneration extended beyond this life, as part of filial duty was to revere the dead. Following one's death, there was the belief that the soul did not ascend to heaven but continued to exist, albeit unseen, on earth. Moreover, one's duty extended beyond the need to maintain harmony between heaven and earth and included the pacification of ancestors through ritual worship. As villages began to develop, particular ancestors and gods were incorporated into the locale's pantheon, and annual festivals honoring these unseen beings added to the strength of the community in early Vietnam. These local festivals are still part of Vietnam's village life.

Vietnamese point back to the kingdom of Van Lang as its golden age, when sage-kings ruled the Red River area. Also known as the Dong Sonian culture, this period extended from the seventh century B.C. to the founding of the Au Lac state in the third century B.C.

The last three centuries B.C. in Vietnam witnessed an increased use of iron tools and weaponry. One consequence of this development was greater production in agriculture, as iron plows broke up hard soil. Monsoon season and a delta area that was basically at sea level necessitated an intricate network of dikes and irrigation canals to maintain proper water levels for the all-important crop of rice.

Rice Culture

We should stop here to note the implications of a rice-based culture. Rice is what makes some nations rich and others poor; it unites and divides societies; it sustains large populations and is often used as the basis of taxation.

Vietnam's society was centered on rice cultivation. This agricultural endeavor required group effort because it was extremely labor-intensive. Growing rice demanded that land be shaped into flat paddies that could be flooded and drained. It was imperative that the water level in the paddy remained at a particular level during the planting, growing, and harvesting periods. Vietnamese would plant the rice one stalk at a time and harvest it in the same manner. Following the harvest, the crop had to be dried, and then the seed separated from the husk. With such an undertaking we can understand why the earliest villages and clans developed around the rice-fields. Economically, this grain was important because it could be stored, which meant that there was food during the monsoon season, when it was impossible to fish or cultivate the ground. Increased prosperity due to rice-agriculture gave rise to other economic endeavors, including animal husbandry and trade with neighboring states.

These rice-producing areas along the Red River became known as Lac fields, and those who owned large fields were called Lac lords. Vietnamese claim that prior to the third century B.C. Hung kings reigned over the Lac lords. It is probable that the king held his position on the basis of his wealth, and while he did not demand taxes from the other Lac lords, he was showered with gifts from these subordinate landowners.

Qin China (221–206 B.C.)

Vietnam's stability and growth was threatened by ominous changes in China. For most of the first millennium B.C., Vietnam's northern neighbor was wracked with incessant wars

It takes a community to grow rice because, among other reasons, the paddies' water levels must be regulated. Here, two men transfer water from one paddy to another.

Three generations in the rice field.

between various states. This period of Chinese history is termed the "Warring States Period." However, the Qin State's power grew during the fourth and third centuries and, by 221 B.C, Qin had conquered its enemies and created a unified polity. Fearful of what a united China meant for business, many non-Chinese aristocratic families fled to areas outside of China, including the southern state of Nan Yueh (Nam Viet). Lac lords united with these new economically powerful northerners and created unified political institutions. One result of this union was the establishment of a much stronger southern state known as Au Lac.

King An Duong was the founder of this state, and the first Vietnamese figure that is verified in historical documents. In 258 B.C. King Duong defeated his rivals in the Red River Delta area, and he built his capital at Co Loa, thirty-five kilometers north of present-day Hanoi.

Au Lac signified a more unified state. However, the Qin dynasty, led by Emperor Shi Huangdi, continued to conquer its southern neighbors. General Trieu Da led the Qin army into Vietnam and defeated the Au Lac king at Coa Loa, thereby incorporating Vietnam into the Qin state. Flush with victory, General Trieu Da made plans to return north until he was informed that his emperor, Shi Huangdi, had died and that the Han state had defeated the Qin in the north and established the Han Dynasty (207 B.C.–221 A.D.).

Presented with various options, the Chinese general chose to create an independent state in southern China with a capital at Canton. He divided this autonomous state into various regions, of which Vietnam was a part. One might think that General Trieu Da would be a villain in Vietnamese history, but he is celebrated as an individual who stood up against Han intentions to incorporate Vietnam into the Chinese empire.

THE CHINESE MILLENNIUM
(111 B.C.–939 A.D.)

The Shaping of Vietnam's World

China's Han Empire was an amazing display of political, military, and economic power. It was just a matter of time until its influence was spread south and, in 111 B.C., the Han army conquered Vietnam and integrated it into its empire. For the next 1,000 years, the Vietnamese would be under China's rule. It is difficult, if not impossible, to grasp the many implications of China's millennium of political dominance in Vietnam. Rather than presenting this section of Vietnam's history chronologically, it might be best to present four themes that shaped Chinese-Vietnamese relations during this period.

Confucianism as a Worldview

Some historians estimate that more human beings have been influenced by the doctrines of the Chinese scholar Kong Fuzi ("Master Kong") than by any other teachings. We know this teacher as Confucius (551–479). Confucianism helped shape the Vietnamese worldview. Thus, if we wish to understand Vietnam we must study the Confucian principles.

    Born in northeast China to a family that ranked among the nobility, Confucius grew up in a land marked by competing

先師孔子行教像

德佈天地 道冠古今
刪述六經 垂憲萬世

Confucius (551–479 B.C.).

states at war with one another. As he grew into adulthood, Confucius believed that peace would prevail between states if people would follow his teachings. He did not claim to be enlightened or heaven-sent, and he did not report a particular epiphany or conversion experience. He noted that he was not teaching anything new, but was simply explaining what earlier sage-kings had lived and taught.

Confucius followed the ancient paradigm of a tri-level view of the cosmos: heaven, earth, and humanity. He taught that it was man's (he was chauvinistic in his worldview) duty to make sure that harmony was kept between heaven and earth. He also proclaimed that human virtue would create harmony and produce peace between warring states.

Confucius taught that two elements were absolutely necessary for virtue. First, it was imperative that rituals be conducted according to the prescribed teachings of China's earlier sage-kings, doctrines that were revealed in ancient texts. Confucius did not have to resurrect these ancient Chinese texts because they had been revered for generations. However, he highlighted the nature of ritual in these writings and commented on what these old texts taught about proper ceremony. One analyst uses the example of a handshake to illustrate what Confucius meant by appropriate ritual. The manner by which one shakes hands with another person might convey a host of feelings: anger, joy, affection, or empathy. Similarly, Confucius believed that it was not enough to perform a ritual, one needed to do it with proper emotions and conduct.

Along with proper action in performing rites, Confucius taught that virtue was based on the proper maintenance of five social relationships: ruler-subject, father-son, husband-wife, older brother-younger brother, and friend-friend. In the first four relationships there is a definite superior-subordinate role of each player: a subject is required to be faithful to the ruler; a son must demonstrate filial piety to his father; a wife is the servant of her husband; and a younger brother must defer to his older brother. Confucius maintained that peace would prevail in a society where everyone accepted his or her role. The basis for this hierarchy of social and political relationships was that it was the will of heaven.

Moreover, a society should follow the will of its emperor because heaven has placed him on the throne. To rebel against the emperor was to reject the mandate of heaven—and heaven's punishment could be severe. As the mediator between heaven and earth, the emperor's primary responsibilities were to be virtuous and to make annual sacrifices and prayers to heaven. If an emperor failed to carry out his duties, he could incur heaven's wrath. This displeasure would manifest itself through natural disasters, famine, and pestilence. According to Mencius, a later disciple of Confucius, if a ruler loses heaven's blessing, society must depose that ruler.

In Vietnam, this philosophy provided a paradigm for a political order. Vietnamese viewed their emperor as an individual that heaven had put on the throne. Not merely a symbolic figure, the emperor also directed the bureaucracy.

Daoism as a Worldview

There was another worldview that developed in China and eventually made its way into Vietnam. As a reaction against the stringent form of Confucianism, a school of thought formed

History is important in a Confucian society. Here, a man points to an ancient text in Hanoi's History Museum.

around the teachings of Lao Tzu, a historical figure alleged to have lived in the sixth century B.C. His pithy sayings, written in the *Dao Di Qing*, focused on the importance of heart-felt attitudes over the mechanistic forms of Confucian ritual. Daoists ridiculed the Confucian scholars' hypocrisy because Confucius taught that human beings should not be concerned with the afterworld; yet, Confucian teachers created elaborate (and expensive) funeral rituals to placate the souls of the deceased.

For the Daoists, life is to be enjoyed by letting nature take its course. A popular Daoist proverb claims that "The one who knows does not speak; the one who speaks does not know." Using the analogy of water, Daoists point out that this soft matter, by just following its nature, is able to carve out entire mountains. Daoism is also much more mystical than Confucianism. Practicing Daoists seek to live long lives through incantations, potions, sexual practices, meditation, and breathing exercises. Believing that the world is charged with energy, Daoist temples are built to honor numerous deities, including Lao Tzu, who had achieved divine status by the first century B.C.

In Vietnam, Daoism did not displace Confucianism. But it was, and still is, common to see a Vietnamese village with a Daoist shrine connected to it. Daoism was adopted as an alternative worldview for the Vietnamese in answer to the numerous calamities that they endured. Domestically, the devastation that occurred from yearly monsoon floods was tragic. Annual torrential rains damaged crops, destroyed homes, and caused human suffering. In addition, Vietnam experienced rancorous international relations. Bloody wars characterized the history of Vietnam, and the teachings of the Dao brought comfort to the Vietnamese as they endured hardship knowing that, in the end, the water destroys the mountain.

Buddhism as a Worldview

During China's millennium-long rule, Buddhism was the foreign religion that made the greatest and most lasting impact on Vietnamese society. At the outset of the twenty-first century, ninety percent of Vietnamese claim to be Buddhists. Vietnam played a pivotal role in the spread of Buddhism to East and Southeast Asia because it provided a central location where South Asian Buddhist missionaries and Chinese monks could congregate. Along the coasts of northern Vietnam, foreign Buddhist merchants established trading bases and their communities also became stations for Buddhist missionaries. Obviously, Buddhism did not just pass through Vietnam or remain on the periphery—eventually it was so completely embraced that it became the nation's official religion.

Sidhartha Gautema (560–483), the son of a north Indian royal family, is the founder of Buddhism. As a young man, Sidhartha eschewed the comforts of the palace life and set out on a journey to find the reality behind human existence. He eventually achieved enlightenment and began to spread the good news. Paradoxically, the good news was bad news. According to the Buddha, the primary reality is that sorrow defines all existence. Following this first noble truth is the principle that the source of all sorrow is desire. For orthodox Buddhists, life is spent trying to empty desire from one's self. If selfishness remains, then the individual is reborn into this world of misery. Merit (karma) accrued in this life will enhance one's chances of enlightenment in the next life.

The Buddha explained an eight-fold path that aids humanity on the corridor to enlightenment. This path includes directives for right speech, right occupation, and the cultivation of compassion.

In orthodox Buddhism, the eventual goal is not eternal life or an eternity in heaven, but a life of enlightenment after which one ceases to exist on the wheel of birth and rebirth. The death of an enlightened being is pictured as the snuffing out of a candle or the fall of a raindrop into the ocean.

Following the Buddha's death, disputes about his teachings divided his followers and two major Buddhist schools emerged: the Theravada (orthodox) school and the Mahayana (unorthodox) school. The Mahayana school made its way across the mountains into China. In southern India, missionaries spread the orthodox message to neighboring Ceylon (Sri Lanka), Burma (Myanmar), and other portions of Southeast Asia. Both these schools of Buddhism were brought to Vietnam.

While there were adherents to the Theravada school, it was the unorthodox branch that made major inroads into Vietnamese society. Vietnamese chose Mahayana Buddhism because it allowed them to incorporate indigenous beliefs and local deities into the foreign religion. Some also speculate that Mahayana doctrines received legitimacy in Vietnam because they came by way of China—a country that culturally dominated Asia.

The most popular form of Mahayana Buddhism was from the Chan School or Zen Buddhism, despite its rigorous discipline of mediation and self-control. In later centuries, the Pure Land form of Buddhism became popular in Vietnam. Pure Land doctrine asserts that salvation comes from placing faith in the righteousness of the Buddha Amida, who lived on the earth in early times. Practitioners of this form of Buddhism repeatedly recite a brief prayer wherein they acknowledge faith in the Buddha Amida and request that his righteousness be imputed to them.

Prayers being offered in a local Buddhist temple; Mahayana Buddhism is the country's dominant religion.

A Vietnamese monk carries a bowl into which the general public can place rice and other foodstuffs.

There are many reasons why the Vietnamese accepted the teachings of Buddhism and why it has remained the state religion. First, the Vietnamese observed that outside powers, whether China or India, had a more sophisticated culture and society. So when these foreigners brought with them a different religion, the Vietnamese took notice. Moreover, the religion that the Buddhist Chinese and Indian monks introduced to the Vietnamese was more elaborate in rituals than the animistic-based indigenous beliefs. The Buddhism that was introduced to the Vietnamese included sacred texts, an organized church, mantras, robes, and ornate artwork. As noted earlier, the opportunity to integrate indigenous beliefs with the unorthodox Buddhism also facilitated the spread of this alien religion throughout Vietnam.

Furthermore, karma is an attractive feature of Buddhism for the Vietnamese because this concept allows human beings to explain hardship, and Vietnam has experienced much sorrow in its history.

Scholars and a Chinese-Style Bureaucracy

Before the Chinese incorporated it into a much larger bureaucracy, Vietnam's political structure was quite loose. Lac lords were the economic elite in Vietnam, and they acknowledged the king by sending gifts to his capital. Upon their arrival, the Chinese recognized the importance of the Lac lords and provided them with seals and ribbons. This sanction was a mixed blessing for the Lac lords. For while they enjoyed the recognition that the Chinese gave them, they were now part of a bureaucracy. As such, they were required to collect taxes and maintain order in their lands.

Confucian influence on Vietnamese society grew during the first millennium A.D., one consequence of which was the formation of a scholarly elite. Mencius, the aforementioned disciple of Confucius, taught that there were two types of men (he was as chauvinistic as Confucius): one group that worked with their minds, and another that worked with their hands. He also believed that every man was born with the same academic potential, but that most men were lazy and did not exercise their minds. More importantly, he elaborated upon Confucius' teaching that a virtuous society was one where men who worked with their minds ruled over those that chose to work with their hands.

As a result of these thoughts, an examination system was created in China wherein men would be tested on their knowledge of classic Chinese books, their calligraphy, and their ability to express themselves in essay form. The very few that passed these arduous exams received coveted government posts. This system was ostensibly egalitarian because any man, no matter his economic position, had an opportunity to prove himself at the annual exam. In reality, the individuals who passed these exams were usually the sons of government officials and the offspring of the wealthy. Only government officials and the rich could afford to send their sons to tutors and schools where they could learn calligraphy and the material needed to pass the exams. An elite scholarly class, also known as mandarins, held the reigns of political, social, and economic power in China.

This examination system was adopted in Vietnam. Vietnamese who wished to be part of the Chinese-controlled government in their land had to study the Chinese classics and prepare for an exam that emphasized Chinese learning. If they passed these exams, they would join the bureaucracy and would be touted as the most virtuous of men. The men who passed these exams were so honored in Vietnam that when villagers heard that one of its sons had passed it, celebrations would occur and they would construct a special home for the man's family.

One effect of the mandarin system was stability in the government. While emperors and outside aggressors would come and go, at the center was an elite scholarly class that the Vietnamese rank-and-file would look to for guidance. This system would also create problems for future visionaries who tried to implement Socialism, Communism, and Democracy in Vietnam's society. At the same time, the mandarin system was so ingrained in the Vietnamese world that various imperialist powers would seek to use this paradigm to legitimize their control of Vietnam.

China's Sweet and Sour Rule in Vietnam

China's success in controlling Vietnam was connected to the vigor and stability of the Chinese empire. Paradoxically, the stronger the Chinese court, the more problems the Chinese had in Vietnam. In fact, the Chinese exerted intense control in Vietnam only when China was flourishing and they had the military and political power to back up their demands on the southern states. During good times in China, the majority of the Chinese who came to Vietnam were soldiers and bureaucrats who intended to get rich quick and then return home. However, when China was weak, there was stability in Vietnam because its northern overlord's policy was less intrusive. When China was in chaos, the Chinese who moved in to Vietnam were usually aristocratic families hoping to protect their possessions. These elite Chinese families moved to Vietnam with the intention of making it their home, intermarrying with the Vietnamese and adopting Vietnamese culture.

It should be noted that there were several Vietnamese revolutions during China's rule in the area. Lac lords cooperated with Han officials during the first decades of Chinese rule in Vietnam, but eventually the Lac lords grew to resent Chinese intrusion and the new taxes they were required to pay.

A woman led the first major rebellion against Chinese rule. The wife of a disgruntled Lac lord, Trung Trac gathered an army around her in 42 A.D. and pushed out the Han prefect in Vietnam. After her victory, Lac lords supported Trung Trac and returned to the economic system where no taxes were required. When the Chinese returned with an army of 20,000, however, many of her supporters abandoned her. According to legend, the Chinese captured Trung Trac and her sister, Nhi, and sent their heads back to China as victorious trophies. However, Vietnamese sources claim that Trung Trac and Nhi committed suicide rather than surrender to the Chinese.

Two remarkable Vietnamese revolts against China occurred during the sixth century. Ly Bi, a descendent of a Chinese family who had earlier moved to Vietnam, rebelled against China in 543 and declared himself emperor of Van Xuan (10,000 Springs). It took the Chinese four years to respond, but when they did it was decisive. They defeated Ly Bi's army and, while he was retreating, he was ambushed and killed by mountain tribesmen. Vietnamese history records that Ly Bi's followers continued to resist the Chinese for the next half century.

During 546, after Li Bi's withdrawal from the advancing Chinese army, Trieu Quang Phuc led an army of 20,000 against the Chinese. The son of a noted scholar, his strategy was to attack the Chinese army at night and then retreat into the dense swamps to rest during the day. His tactics were effective and the Chinese general claimed that the swamps were the home of bandits. Quang Phuc's reputation grew with the Vietnamese and he proclaimed himself the king of Da Trach, "King of the Night Marsh." His ascendancy to leadership was facilitated by Ly Bi's defeat, after which point Ly Bi's followers joined Quang Phuc's army. Also, the Chinese general had to return to China to address domestic crises in his homeland.

Vietnamese legends claim that Quang Phuc installed an altar in the swamp and offered prayers and incense to heaven. His prayers were answered and he was given the claw of a yellow dragon and told to place the claw in his helmet to be assured of victory. Quang Phuc's rebellion had many indigenous overtones. He proclaimed himself king, not emperor, which demonstrated his alliance with earlier rulers in Vietnam. He was not descended from a Chinese family as Ly Bi had been, and the metaphysical elements of his story coincide with the Vietnamese notion that a ruler should possess heaven-sent metaphysical power. Quang Phuc's rebellion could not dislodge Chinese rule in Vietnam, but he is celebrated in Vietnam as a hero who fought foreign aggression. He is not mentioned in Chinese records.

The Persistence of Vietnamese Culture

A final theme to note about Chinese-Vietnamese relations is the strength and richness of Vietnam's culture. It is difficult to fathom how a country can be politically and socially dominated by another country for 1,000 years and emerge with its culture intact. Language and the position of women are two

Vietnamese institutions that refused to completely conform to the Chinese pattern.

Language in Vietnam

For a millennium the knowledge of Chinese language was a requirement for any Vietnamese government employee. The all-important mandarin class communicated in Chinese, and so the language held a distinctive position in Vietnam's society. Yet, despite the official role of Chinese in Vietnam, the Vietnamese language remained the lingua franca of the population. To be sure, many Chinese words were borrowed in making up the Vietnamese language, but the fact is that the Vietnamese language endured despite the status given to Chinese. Also, rather than a wholesale incorporation of Chinese writing, the Vietnamese created a popular script wherein they used Chinese characters to standardize a phonetic pattern. Known as *chu nom* ("southern character"), this new script began in the eighth century and was fully developed by the thirteenth century.

The Role of Women in Vietnam

Historically, Chinese civilization is male-centered. Women were most valued for their ability to produce sons. Men who could afford it had multiple wives, concubines, and consorts. A wife who was intimate with a man, other than her husband, was put to death. Chinese women were to be obedient to their fathers, and then to their husbands. If her husband predeceased her, she then owed her obedience to her eldest son. A distinctive feature of Confucianism is the perpetuation of the subordinate role women are to play in society. In imperial China, only men

The earliest Chinese writings are found on oracle bones such as these. The Vietnamese borrowed the character-based writing system from China, and it was not until the sixteenth century that a romanized system of writing was introduced.

owned property, and eternal life was synonymous with continuing the family name through sons.

When the Chinese came to Vietnam, they met a society where women were not the slaves of men. When a Vietnamese woman married a man, she did not lose her identity. Vietnamese husbands became as much a part of their wives' families as their own. Vietnamese wives inherited the property of their deceased husbands, and they had the right to divorce them.

A priority for the early Chinese officials in Vietnam was to transform the gender relationship among the Vietnamese and make it conform to the Chinese pattern. When the Vietnamese refused to change, the Chinese tried to bribe the men. They offered property to every Vietnamese male who would undergo a Chinese wedding ceremony. The Chinese believed that if they could transform the wedding ceremony into the Chinese pattern, then the entire marriage would come to mirror the Chinese model. A Chinese marriage ceremony symbolizes a patriarchal worldview where a woman loses all connection with her parents. Vietnamese men took advantage of the property offers in exchange for a Chinese wedding, but the role of Vietnamese women did not change during China's tenure there. When Chinese rule finally ended in its extreme southern provinces, it did so knowing that it had not transformed the Vietnamese family or the role of Vietnamese women in society.

Following their engagement, a Vietnamese couple takes a boat ride with family members.

Vietnam's Transition To Independence

The Battle of Bach Dang River (938)

The Tang Dynasty (618–907) was China's golden age. Its splendor and that of its capital Changan were so well known throughout Asia that Japan, Korea, and Vietnam rebuilt their capital cities to imitate the glorious structures in Changan. But as the glory of Tang China faded in the early tenth century, an opportunity for independence presented itself to the Vietnamese.

Vietnamese General Ngo Quyen organized an indigenous army to gain Vietnam's autonomy. Ngo Quyen was the son of a provincial official and was raised near the western Red River Delta. In 937 he attacked the Chinese army and prepared for an impending naval battle. He did this by placing wooden poles in the bed of the Bach Dang River—the passageway into Vietnam at the entrance to the Tonkin Gulf. The Vietnamese leader ordered that these poles be embedded at a height just under the water surface at high tide. When the Chinese navy arrived, they were lured into the mouth of the Bach Dang River during high tide. When the tide ebbed, the Chinese boats were impaled on the poles. Thus the Vietnamese routed the Chinese invading force.

The Battle of Bach Dang River in 938 is celebrated as the beginning of Vietnamese independence from China. Following this engagement, Ngo Quyen declared himself king of an independent Nam Viet. His choice of Co Loa as his state's capital was extremely symbolic. Just north of Hanoi, this municipality had been Vietnam's headquarters prior to the Chinese invasion of Vietnam. Ngo Quyen was more successful on the battlefield, however, than he was in the palace. When he died in 944 at the age of forty-seven, Vietnam's political landscape was marked by instability. Dinh Bo Linh filled the power vacuum that developed in Vietnam.

Dinh Bo Linh (r. 965–979)

King Dinh Bo Linh, founder of the Dinh dynasty.

Dinh Bo Linh was atypical of the leaders to which Vietnam had grown accustomed. The Chinese system prescribed that officials should demonstrate scholarly prowess. However, this was not the case with Bo Linh. The product of an illicit affair, Bo Linh was raised in a village along the Red River Delta. His early years were spent guarding the area's water buffaloes. As a young man his charismatic personality vaulted him into the village leadership position. Eventually he became the military leader of the region.

Following Ngo Quyen's death, Bo Linh defeated all his potential rivals and established the Dinh dynasty. He moved the capital from the open plain area of Co Loa to Hoa Lu, located farther from China and surrounded by mountains. Hoa Lu was chosen because it was an area that was easy to defend.

This event marks a shift in Vietnam's political paradigm. Prior to Bo Linh, rulers in Vietnam chose the open plain areas for their capitals because these lands were conducive to large-scale agriculture adventures. Moreover, there was a sense that heaven had placed a ruler on the throne, and so legitimization was not solely based on military might. Bo Linh did not have scholarly credentials, however, and his power was justified solely by his military victories. Consequently, his choice of Hoa Lu demonstrated that his rule was based on his military expertise.

While he consolidated regional power, Bo Linh kept a wary eye on China because it was reemerging as a united polity that would eventually be known as the Song dynasty. He sent a tribute mission to the Song court with the hope that they would recognize the independent state of Dai Co Viet (Great Viet). To demonstrate his subordination to China, he made it clear that the ruler of Dai Co Viet would take the title of king and not emperor. Song officials recognized the independent state of Dai Co Viet, being too busy with domestic issues to worry about former peripheral states. Despite China's recognition of his state, Bo Linh created a 100,000-man army, whose structure reached down to local militias. The emphasis on a strong military would remain in Vietnam long after Linh passed from the scene.

A large army did not prevent an implosion in Vietnam's political world following Bo Linh's death. Indeed, the early tenth century attempts at Vietnamese indigenous rule ended in failure. In retrospect, Bo Linh and Ngo Quyen are best understood as transitional figures in Vietnam's political history. The Vietnamese needed these brief dynasties to throw off

Pillars found at the ancient Vietnamese capital of Hoa–Lu.

the Chinese political paradigm. It would not be until the year 1009, under the leadership of Ly Cong Uan, that Vietnam would find its political bearings and establish an independent dynasty that would endure.

The Ly Dynasty (1009–1225)

Like the first wobbly steps of an infant, Vietnam's first decades of independence from China were marked by fits and starts. Two vital issues that needed to be addressed during this transition period were the type of relationship an independent Vietnam would have with China; and the source of a king or emperor's right to rule Vietnam. The institution that resolved both of these issues was the Buddhist Church. Vietnamese monks from the Buddhist temples enjoyed regular contact with their colleagues across land and water borders. Moreover, as potential leaders came to the fore in an independent Vietnam, they would use the monks to serve as mediators between Vietnam and China. Because of their interaction with their Chinese colleagues, Vietnamese monks understood Chinese protocol and were of great service to the fledgling indigenous Vietnamese kingdoms.

The Deva-Raja

More importantly, tenth-century Vietnamese monks were heavily influenced by the teachings brought from southern states. This region was marked by a syncretic doctrinal system that included aspects of Theravada Buddhism, Animism, and Hinduism. Emerging out of this amalgam was the principle of the *deva-raja*, or god-king. Some observers call it the theory of the great-man, wherein an individual's physical and spiritual prowess legitimates his rule. Moreover, it was usually the Buddhist monks who verified that an individual possessed miraculous powers and the mandate of heaven to rule. It therefore behooved every aspirant to the throne to receive the blessings and confirmation of rule by the Buddhist Church.

Ly Thai To (r. 1010–1028)

Ly Cong Uan (974–1028) was born into this evolving political world. Reportedly an orphan raised in a Buddhist monastery, the monks secured Ly Cong Uan a position as a palace guard at Hoa Lu. Following the death of Bo Linh and the subsequent rule of incompetent kings, the clerics used their influence to place Ly Cong Uan on the throne. He established the Ly dynasty (1009–1225) and gave himself the name Ly Thai To.

Following the founding of this dynasty, Ly Thai To moved the capital from the relatively remote area of Hoa Lu back to the large fields near modern-day Hanoi. He gave his new capital the name Thang Long (soaring dragon) because he reportedly saw a dragon rising to the sky as he approached the area. The fact that Ly Thai To moved the capital to an open region demonstrated that he received legitimacy from heaven rather than from military power. Once established at Thang Long, the emperor reorganized Vietnam's territory into districts and created a bureaucracy to help manage the state. His tax policy was lenient toward the common farmer, perhaps because his own beginnings were so humble. He was a devout Buddhist and built elaborate places of worship as well as monasteries where monks educated individuals to work in his government.

Vietnamese Chams in a traditional festival. Cham peoples are one of the fifty–three ethnic groups in Vietnam.

Once he achieved economic and political stability, Ly Thai To turned his attention to expanding his empire at the expense of the southern Cham and Cambodian kingdoms. The mostly acrimonious relationship Vietnam had with its southern neighbors eventually resulted in three Cham provinces being ceded to Vietnam in 1078. During the fifteenth century, Vietnam completely defeated the Champa kingdom. As shown further below, the invasion and destruction of the Cambodian kingdoms created an animosity between the Vietnamese and Cambodians that would continue into the twentieth century.

Ly Phat Ma (r. 1028–1054)

Ly Thai To, who died in 1028, laid the foundation for one of Vietnam's greatest dynasties. His main failure was in not addressing the usual chaos that surrounded the transition of power after an emperor's death. Four sons fought each other for the throne with Ly Phat Ma, posthumously known as Ly Thai Tong, emerging as the victor. He ascended to power at the age of twenty-eight, and went on to rule from 1028 to 1054. He is now recognized as the emperor that brought the Ly dynasty to its political height. A devout follower of the Zen sect of Buddhism, Ly Phat Ma continued his father's policy of gathering advisors from the Buddhist monasteries. Because of the domestic battles for the throne, the emperor began to transfer the responsibility of governing from the extended royal family to large landowners. He maintained a strong army to wage battles with Champa and to discourage relatives from plotting his overthrow. His policies brought peace to Vietnam and, following his death in 1054, there was a peaceful transition of power to his son, Ly Thanh Tong.

Ly Thanh Tong (r. 1054–1072)

The third Ly emperor secured even more prestigious victories over Champa. During a major offensive in 1068, Vietnamese soldiers sacked Champa's capital and captured its king. At the domestic level, Ly Thanh Tong actively promoted Confucianism. In 1072, two years before his death, he commanded that a temple be built in honor of Chinese literature. The structure was used as a school to train government officials.

Ly Can Duc (r. 1072–1127)

Ly Can Duc was the fourth emperor during the Ly dynasty. He is considered the last strong Ly emperor. Under his rule the examination system was established in Thang Long, which created a stronger bureaucracy. He ruled for fifty-six years and, following his death, Ly emperors increasingly relied on their advisors to rule for them.

During the Ly dynasty China attempted to reassert its influence on Vietnam. The battles between them were indecisive, forcing China to acknowledge that it had an autonomous southern neighbor. For its part, Vietnam continued to recognize China's prestige by sending tribute to China.

Tran Dynasty (1225–1400)

During the final years of the Ly dynasty, the Ly emperor was, in essence, the puppet of Tran advisors. Members of the Tran clan were the most powerful court advisors. Eventually, the Tran family grew tired of leading behind the scenes and, in 1225, they had members of the imperial family killed. Once the Tran dynasty was established, its leaders set out to correct the political weaknesses that had led to their predecessor's fall.

Three Changes in Court Politics

First, the Tran recognized that the Ly dynasty had grown weak because its emperors had chosen their brides from outside clans. Thus relatives of the brides often exercised inordinate power in the imperial court. In fact, this is how the Tran had found an entrance into the Ly court. Tran emperors were not about to make this same mistake, and they instituted a policy wherein brides could be chosen only from within their own clan. In this way, maternal relatives would pose less of a threat to the throne's stability because it would be in their interest to support the Tran family.

Tran emperors also understood the importance of not leaving the throne to a child who could be easily manipulated. Moreover, emperors began the practice of abdicating to serve as "senior kings" once their predecessor died, thus allowing the next generation to establish itself at court.

Tran advisors recognized that another failure of the Ly court was that it had allowed outside families to farm large tracts of land around the capital. While the Ly dynasty relied solely on the Buddhist Church to authenticate its rule, Tran advisors believed that to govern successfully there had to be economic power behind the throne. Consequently, they confiscated the farms around the capital and placed them in the hands of court family members. This two-edged policy dismantled local rivals and increased the court's economic power.

A third policy shift during Tran Vietnam was the increased sophistication of the examination system. Multiple degrees placed candidates at various levels of an increasingly complicated bureaucracy. There were five major books that the candidates were to study for the state exams, known as the Confucian classics. The first book, entitled *Yijing* (*Book of Changes*), consists of pithy texts that give clues to those that seek answers through divination. Vietnamese scholars also studied the *Book of History*. Based on reports from kings that lived during China's Shang (1500–1066) and early Chou (1122–476) periods, this book supposedly contains the sage advice of China's cultural heroes. The third book that candidates were examined on is the *Book of Songs*. These are poems, similar to the Hebrew poetry found in the Torah's *Book of Psalms*. They were reportedly written throughout the Shang and Chou eras and were organized by Confucius. The fourth classic is a compilation of texts and is referred to as the *Book of Rites*. As we have seen, Confucianism places a premium on proper ritual and this book explains what this precept entails. Confucius is also credited for arranging these various passages into one text. The final text is directly related to Confucius, and it is known as *The Spring and Autumn Annals*. This book is a concise record of the events in the state of Lu, the home of Confucius, during China's Spring and Autumn period (722 to 481 B.C.). Since China experienced incessant war during this era, the book points out the futility of conflict and the need for China to follow virtuous leaders.

The content of these volumes demonstrate that Vietnamese bureaucrats were steeped in Chinese learning. One could not pass the Vietnamese civil exam without a thorough knowledge of these books. Indeed, one could not even begin to prepare for the exams without a comprehensive ability to read and write in

Chinese. During Tran Vietnam, the influence of Confucianism grew because of the emphasis on Chinese learning and the increased prominence of a bureaucracy based upon it.

Tran advisors instituted the above-noted policies to create domestic stability, and they were successful. Unfortunately, local strength could not prevent external crises. Vietnam faced two major outside threats during the Tran years. The first emergency—the Mongol invasion—boosted Vietnamese confidence in their ability to withstand the invasion of a formidable enemy. However, the Vietnamese then faced an enemy that ended Tran rule and placed Vietnam back in the hands of China.

Foreign Concerns During the Tran Dynasty

The first foreign affairs problem that the Tran emperors had to face came from an unlikely source. For years the Vietnamese had feared the strength of China and the constant danger of renewed hostility with its northern neighbor. In fact, the thirteenth-century invaders that threatened Vietnam came from the north, but they were not Chinese, they were Mongols. Mongolia had an entirely different culture than did China or Vietnam. A sparsely populated region, Mongolia's harsh weather necessitated that its inhabitants eschew a life of farming and exist primarily through ranching. Nomadic clans pushed across the wide range of Mongolia in search of pastureland for their animals.

Regarded as unsophisticated by the Chinese, the Mongols were known for their constant feuding more than for their appreciation of culture. Scholars did not rule the Mongols; rather, as older men became physically weak, they were considered useless in the physically demanding work of ranching. Into this world came Genghis Khan (1162?–1227)—a leader of a

Khubilai Khan (1215–1294).

Mongol clan who eventually united all of Mongolia. History tells the story of the rapid western expansion of the Mongol empire. Yet, Genghis Khan died before his army conquered all of China. Khubilai Khan (1215–1294), the grandson of the Mongolian unifier, did occupy China and established the Yuan dynasty (1271–1368).

The Mongols set their sights further south and Khubilai Khan demanded that the Tran emperor acknowledge Mongol influence over Vietnam. Instead, the Tran court ordered Vietnamese historians to publish a history that emphasized their country's autonomy. Mongol forces responded by invading Vietnamese territory in 1257, 1284, and 1287. Mongol soldiers captured an abandoned Thang Long, but they found out what twentieth-century French and American soldiers would later learn: holding Vietnamese territory does not necessarily mean victory.

Wracked with disease, thin supply lines, and a scorched earth policy that further alienated the Vietnamese population, the Mongols withdrew after their first two invasions. Their final push for Vietnam included an army of 300,000 and a naval flotilla of over 400 ships. Borrowing the tactics of Ngo Quyen, General Tran Hung Dao ordered iron tipped stakes placed in the bed of the Bach Dang River—stakes that would be just below the water surface during high tide. Lured into the mouth of the river by Vietnamese decoys, the Mongol navy found itself stuck when the tide went out and was subsequently destroyed. This victory added to the indigenous legends of Vietnamese triumph over any and every foreign invader.

Vietnam's Tran dynasty followed the cycle of the Ly dynasty: at the outset it was blessed with visionary leaders. But as time went by, prosperity led to softness. Champa, Vietnam's old southern enemy, took advantage of a weak Tran court. During the fourteenth century, Champa invaded Vietnam and looted Thang Long in 1371. Disgusted with the inept Tran court, General Ho Quy Ly seized power and announced the establishment of the Ho dynasty (1400–1407).

Once in power, Ho Quy Ly tried to lessen the influence of Chinese thinking in Vietnam. He limited the amount of land held by the aristocrats, most of whom had ties to Chinese culture. The lands that were confiscated from the rich were distributed to the poor and to social classes that had little connection with China. Ho Quy Ly alienated the scholarly class by ordering that his edicts be written in Vietnamese rather than Chinese. This significant decision demonstrates that by the fifteenth century the Chinese language in Vietnam was principally used only among the officials. Ho Quy Ly's goals were noble, but the rich and the scholars opposed him. Their affinity with China compelled them to request that it send an army to depose Vietnam's anti-Chinese emperor. They did not know what they were asking for!

At the turn of the fifteenth century, China was moving into its apex of power under the Ming dynasty (1368–1644). It welcomed the opportunity to interfere in Vietnamese politics. Sending its army south, the Ming soldiers easily overwhelmed Vietnamese resistance. The seventy-year-old Ho Quy Ly, his son, and other members of his government were shipped back to China where they were made to serve as common soldiers in the

Ming Army. Meanwhile, the Ming emperor took this opportunity to reincorporate Vietnam into China's empire.

For twenty years (1407–1427) harsh Ming governors administered Vietnam as if the country was a province of China. The Vietnamese leadership who requested China's aid quickly found out that they had jumped from the wok into the fire. Many Chinese came to the area with the sole intention of economically exploiting the Vietnamese and then returning north to enjoy Ming China's cultural sophistication. Vietnamese were forced to pay taxes on all products, and forced labor added to the humiliation of outside rule. Even local customs were disrupted by Chinese rule. Hair and clothing styles had to conform to Chinese patterns. Chewing betel nut, a common practice in Vietnam, was forbidden. Despite China's attempt to influence all of Vietnamese life, the only social class thoroughly affected by Ming China rule was that of Vietnamese scholars. The majority of the population continued to teach their children the local language, culture, and folklore.

For all of their pomp, the Chinese effect on Vietnam during this twenty-year period did not successfully alter the Vietnamese worldview. When the foreign Ming politicians and soldiers were defeated in 1428, the Vietnamese settled down to once again enjoy indigenous rule.

Le Loi and the Le Dynasty (1428–1788)

Vietnam's second attachment to the Chinese empire was considerably shorter than its first. After twenty years under Ming China, the Vietnamese were able to break away due to the emergence of the Vietnamese hero, Le Loi (1385–1433).

Le Loi was an official in the Ho administration who resigned his position once the Chinese incorporated Vietnam into the Ming Empire. He returned home and began a local resistance against the Chinese. It was not hard to find anti-Chinese elements because the Ming officials in Vietnam instituted a harsh rule. China intended to stamp its culture onto Vietnam, even if it meant inaugurating a draconian rule over its southern neighbor.

Though there were numerous Vietnamese revolts against Ming rule, Le Loi's band of rebels was the most successful and support flocked to it. Several major battles took place during the 1420s, and by 1428 Le Loi had soundly defeated the Chinese army. Anxious to demonstrate his benevolence, Le Loi allowed the defeated Chinese soldiers and the Vietnamese-based Ming officials to return north. While fighting the Chinese, Le Loi claimed that he fought on behalf of the Tran family and that he intended to place a Tran family member back on the throne once the Chinese withdrew. After he successfully pushed the Chinese out of Vietnam, however, he was pressured into establishing the Le dynasty (1428–1788).

At the outset of his rule, Le Loi discriminately reemployed most of Ho Quy Ly's domestic policies. On the one hand, as a former member of the scholarly elite, Le Loi continued the civil service exam system and the use of Chinese as the official language for court memorials. On the other hand, Le Loi confiscated the large tracts of land that were owned by the aristocrats and instituted a land reform campaign that guaranteed land to even the poorest of Vietnam's farmers. The first three emperors of the Le dynasty continued to follow these policies. Their reigns set the stage for the greatest of the Le emperors, Le Thanh Tong.

Le Thanh Tong (1441–1497)

Le Thanh Tong (r. 1460–1497), greatest of the Le emperors.

During his thirty-seven-year reign, Le Thanh Tong instituted major changes in Vietnam's politics and society. With regard to the government, Le Thanh Tong placed the bureaucracy under the guidance of six ministries: Rites, War, Justice, Interior, Public Works, and Finance. Political power was centered at the court, which further limited the power of the aristocrats. Aware of the inordinate power of the Buddhist Church in Vietnam, Le Thanh Tong made a conscious choice to base his authority and legitimacy on Confucianism rather than Buddhism. Confucianism remained the primary ideology of Le emperors.

Le Thanh Tong attempted to resolve the nagging problem of landlessness among the Vietnamese farmers. Stiff fines were placed on rich landowners who ignored laws regarding the limits of land ownership. Furthermore, the government punished aristocratic families who absconded public lands. Yet, the Vietnamese emperor knew that this alone would not solve the problem of landlessness for the peasants. He instituted programs that opened virgin lands to poor farmers. These regions were made available by the increased network of irrigation canals and the clearing of swamp areas. Moreover, when Vietnam decisively defeated Champa in 1470, Le Thanh Tong created don dien, or military stations, in the south to expedite the flow of the land-less northern populace into the southern region. After political stability in the area was assured, these military stations were turned into villages. The soldiers then moved on and created new frontier posts.

In keeping with a strong centralized government, Le Thanh Tong ordered thorough land and population surveys to be conducted. He believed that it was only in this context that the court could understand what to expect in taxes. He also created a penal code to standardize laws and punishments. The Hong Duc Code (1483) included 721 articles. While these regulations had obvious Confucian overtones, there was a distinct Vietnamese flavor to them. In particular, the code demanded that women possess property rights and enjoy equal inheritance laws with their male counterparts. Women were also given back the right to divorce their husbands. Such laws demonstrated a higher view of women by Vietnamese over and against the more male-centered patterns expressed in Chinese society.

Division at the Court

Following Le Thanh Tong's death, however, weak emperors plagued the Le dynasty. Court intrigue and political conspiracy produced ten emperors in the first thirty years after Le Thanh Tong's death. One reason for the rapid turnaround of emperors was that a non-imperial family, the Mac clan, manipulated its way into court politics. The Mac's inordinate influence on the Le emperors eventually led to an outright seizure of the throne, with Mac Dang Dung ousting the Le emperor in 1527. That same year he declared the founding of the Mac dynasty (1527–1592). Though the Le family was weak, Confucian ideals

Vietnamese slowly migrated into southern Vietnam following the demise of the Champa state. This market is located on the Han River, in the capital city of the Can Tho Province.

prompted several aristocratic families to reject Mac leadership and to declare their support for the ousted Le emperor.

Nguyen Kim (1467–1545) led the anti-Mac contingent. He was a court official who was related by marriage to the Le family. Six years after Mac Dang Dung deposed the Le emperor, Nguyen Kim supported the ousted Le chief, Le Trang Ton, who declared himself the legitimate ruler of Vietnam. The royal Le family was exiled to Laos, and Nguyen Kim battled the Mac forces so that the Le contingent could return to rule Vietnam. Following initial Nguyen victories, the Le emperor returned to Vietnam and set up court in Thanh Hoa Province, which is south of the Red River Delta. Members of the Mac dynasty finally killed Nguyen Kim in 1545—presumably by poisoning his food.

Nonetheless, the Nguyen family continued to fight the Mac emperor. Trinh Kien, a son-in-law of Nguyen Kim, became the leading figure at the Le court. Meanwhile, Nguyen Hoang, a son of Nguyen Kim, was assigned to govern Vietnam's southern provinces of Thuan Hoa and Quang Nam. While Trinh Kiem and Nguyen Hoang were wary of each other, they agreed to cooperate and reestablished the Le dynasty in 1592.

One might guess that, though the Le emperor was restored to power, the real ruling force was with the Trinh and Nguyen contingents. Unfortunately, rivalries between Trinh and Nguyen leadership grew into acrimonious relations and eventually into full-scale war. An ominous split between the North and the South resulted. In later centuries, foreign armies would use this division to justify their exploitation of Vietnam.

In the Trinh (North) and Nguyen (South) rivalry, it appeared that the North enjoyed many advantages over its southern foe. The northern Red River Delta area was where Vietnam's civilization began. Moreover, it was the economic and

The Thien Mu Pagoda was built by Nguyen Hoang in 1601. Each of its seven tiers represents a reincarnation of Buddha.

Interior of Dai Hung Temple at Thien Mu Pagoda.

urban center of Vietnam. Since the South was less developed economically, the Vietnamese that migrated to the region were usually poor farmers hoping to eke out a living on Vietnam's southern frontier. Trinh lords in the North created a formidable army of 100,000 soldiers, 500 elephants, and a navy with over 500 vessels.

Yet, the Nguyen held their own in this civil war due to three factors. First, the local population was eager to defend its lands. Much like the South in the U.S. Civil War, the southerners fought tenaciously to hold on to their institutions and lands. Second, the vast open lands in the Mekong Delta that the Vietnamese gained in their war with Champa was fertile soil for farming. This land attracted a range of characters, including over 3,000 Chinese who fled from China's new Manchu-led Qing dynasty (1644–1912). Finally, though inferior to the Trinh in numbers, the Nguyen were superior to their northern enemy in terms of weapon sophistication. This is because the Europeans more readily aided the Nguyen in this civil war.

Thus, the Nguyen contingent held its own in this civil war. After two major battles in 1661 and 1672, the Trinh and Nguyen families settled down to a century-long truce. It was during this respite from fighting that the Europeans maneuvered to increase their influence in Vietnam.

Western Presence in Vietnam

Silks and Spices

Since Vietnam has experienced so much disruption from the West, it would be helpful to understand what brought these foreigners to Vietnam. From the era of the Roman Empire, western traders made their way to Vietnam. Though their primary interest was to buy the amazing silk products made in China, they found that they could reach China through a water route with occasional stops in Vietnam. Following the fall of the Roman Empire, there was a decrease in East-West interaction. However, with the rise of the Moslem empires in the tenth and eleventh centuries, spices from the Far East began to make their way into European markets. Europeans particularly sought three spices: nutmeg, clove, and mace. These products were exclusively found in the Mollucus islands in what is now Indonesia. Alexandria, Baghdad, and Constantinople were three locations west of India where nutmeg, clove, and mace were sold. While these first two cities were under Moslem rule, the Christian city of Constantinople allowed Europeans to purchase these precious seasoning products. All of this changed in 1453, when Constantinople was incorporated into the expanding Islamic empire. The Moslems now enjoyed a monopoly in spice trade. Not only did they raise the price of spices, but they also instructed the Christians that the only two cities where this commodity could be purchased were Venice and Genoa.

The hard bargain that the Moslems placed on spice-trade was a primary motive for Europeans to once again become interested in Asia. It was the small country of Portugal that took the lead in finding a sea route to Asia and, by the early sixteenth century, the Portuguese had established colonies on the western coast of India. In 1511 the Portuguese captured Malacca, an important trading fort on the southern tip of the Malay Peninsula. Because Malacca controlled the traffic through the Malacca Straights, the Portuguese thanked God and their guns for the new land that was theirs. They immediately began to move north to China, Japan, and Vietnam.

Throughout the sixteenth and seventeenth centuries, French, Dutch, English, and Portuguese traders attempted to establish settlements on the Vietnamese coast. By 1700, however, there was a consensus among western merchants that Vietnam offered little promise for profitable commerce. Indeed, Vietnam was inhospitable to the early European merchants. Based on its past, the Vietnamese were wary of any outside power that tried to gain a foothold on its land. They actively discouraged trade with the newly arrived European merchants. Tropical diseases also ravaged early western settlers in Vietnam.

The Jesuits in Vietnam

While merchants abandoned Vietnam, the militant arm of the Catholic Church, the Jesuit missionaries, persevered in bringing their message to the Vietnamese. The three countries in Asia where the Catholic Church garnered the largest percentage of converts were Japan, the Philippines, and Vietnam.

The Christ Monastery in Hue.

In Japan, the expansion of Catholicism was arrested when the Tokugawa government (1603–1868) outlawed this religion at the mid-point of the seventeenth century. The crackdown on the Church in Japan was so successful that it virtually disappeared from the social scene. More than three centuries later, Christians in Japan remain a miniscule percentage of its population.

The opposite occurred in the Philippines. Spain ruled that archipelago from 1565 to 1898. One result of this lengthy rule was that, apart from highland tribes and Moslem communities in the southern islands, most Filipinos embraced this foreign religion.

Vietnam fit somewhere between the two extremes of Japan and the Philippines. Vietnamese did not embrace this religion en masse, but there were royal court members that did convert to Christianity. Catholicism gained a foothold in Vietnam and it remained there.

Alexandre de Rhodes (1591–1660)

One of the first Jesuit missionaries in Vietnam was Alexandre de Rhodes. This French priest had a remarkable gift for learning foreign languages. After six months in Vietnam, he was able to preach in the local language. He would eventually master Chinese, Japanese, Hindustani, and Persian.

In collaboration with several colleagues, Rhodes created a romanized system for writing Vietnamese labeled *quoc ngu*. It simplified the character-based writing that was used by the Vietnamese.

Rhodes was also successful in garnering thousands of converts in the Trinh-dominated section of Vietnam. In fact, so many Vietnamese converted to Christianity under Rhodes' preaching, that the Trinh advisors feared that the religion would undermine political and social stability. For there were certain Christian doctrines that contradicted the worldview of the Vietnamese.

For example, Confucianism teaches that authority rested in the emperor, while the Catholic priests taught that every earthly government was subordinate to the Church. Emperors and wealthy Vietnamese men often practiced polygamy, whereas the Jesuit ministers preached against this custom. In 1630 the Trinh leaders demanded that Rhodes leave their territory. He hoped to continue his work in southern Vietnam, but the Nguyen lords denied him this opportunity there, and he was forced to leave southern Vietnam.

However, using the nearby Portuguese island of Macao as a base, Rhodes repeatedly reentered Vietnam. While he tried to keep a low profile, he was captured several times. During his 1645 trip into Vietnam he was caught by officials and sentenced to death. He languished in prison for weeks while several of his colleagues were executed. Warned not to return to Vietnam, Rhodes received a reprieve from his death sentence and was once again deported.

Rhodes believed that a major hindrance of the Church in Vietnam was that the pope had given the Portuguese priests a ministerial monopoly in this region. By the seventeenth century, Portugal was past its zenith of power in Asia, and the fledgling Catholic work in Vietnam reflected the weakened state of the Portuguese clergy. Rhodes traveled to the Vatican and requested that the pope eliminate the Portuguese authority in the Vietnam Christian Church. His request was denied, and Rhodes returned to France hoping that he could convince French merchants to take a greater interest in Vietnam. While Rhodes' attempts to promote Vietnam as an Asian center of trade failed, the idea of Vietnam as a rich jewel in the French crown was kept alive.

Internal Decay

The first half of the eighteenth century in Vietnam was marked by a truce in the Trinh-Nguyen feud. But the military calm could not hide the growing economic and social problems that both North and South Vietnam faced during this period. Though the North and South were at peace, both camps built up their military forces.

These growing armies were sustained through increased taxation. It was not the rich that bore the brunt of higher taxes. In fact, those that owned the most land—the scholar-officials— were exempt from paying taxes on their property. As a result, a threatening cycle began in Vietnam's countryside. As farmers found it impossible to pay the increased land taxes, they sold their lands to government officials. This newly acquired land would then be exempt from taxes, which further increased the tax burden for the peasants who were trying to hold on to their lands.

Farmers began to neglect the traditional duties of irrigation maintenance because either the land they worked on did not belong to them, or they were so busy trying to pay their taxes, that they had little time for preventative maintenance on dikes and canals. These important waterworks were neglected, resulting in devastating floods that brought famine, death, and disease. Still, the official class grew wealthier, while the peasants struggled to stay alive.

The Tay Son Revolt (1771)

A common response to economic pressure and social injustice is revolt. Between 1730 and 1770, Vietnam witnessed scores of local rebellions. However, none of these were strong enough to threaten the existing political system because the upheavals were geographically confined to local villages. This situation changed with the emergence of the Tay Son brothers.

From the village of Tay Son in the central province of Nghia Binh, three brothers joined forces to overthrow the Nguyen lords. The motivation for this revolt was mixed. Tradition claims that these brothers were offended by the mistreatment of their father at the hands of the Nguyen government. They also were angry because of the Nguyen's penchant for growing rich at the expense of the general population. The popular slogan of the Tay Son rebellion was "seize the property of the rich and distribute it to the poor." Their uprising gained momentum as landless farmers united with the Tay Son army. Together, this force moved south one village at a time.

The Tay Son policy included distributing land and dispersing food from storage bins to the poor. Unlike many of the Nguyen and Trinh lords, the Tay Son brothers allowed the European priests to minister to the Vietnamese populace. As they continued to move toward Gia Dinh (Saigon), the headquarters of the Nguyen leaders, the Tay Son brothers abolished the heavy taxes that burdened the common folk. In 1778 the Nguyen clan was finally defeated by the Tay Son contingent.

Once in Saigon, the Tay Son army vented its fury at Chinese merchants, whom they blamed for exploiting poor Vietnamese. Tay Son soldiers also murdered every member of the ruling

Nguyen family save for Nguyen Anh, the sixteen-year-old nephew of the last Nguyen lord.

Following the Confucian worldview, the Tay Son leaders claimed that they were rebelling in the name of the Le emperor. After they consolidated their lands in the South, the Tay Son generals turned their attention to the North. By 1786 the Tay Son army had destroyed Trinh hegemony in Thang Long, and Vietnam was united under the Tay Son family.

The three brothers installed themselves as kings in the southern, central, and northern divisions of Vietnam. For ceremonial purposes, they pledged their allegiance to the Le emperor, whose court was at the ancient capital of Thang Long (Hanoi). This arrangement lasted only two years. Tired of his ceremonial role, the Le emperor asked China to aid him in overthrowing the Tay Son kings. At the height of its final imperial era, the Qing Dynasty (1644–1912), China responded favorably to the Le emperor's request. A Chinese army of 200,000 soldiers marched into Thang Long and proclaimed that the Le emperor was now the king of Annam.

Nguyen Hue, the second eldest of the Tay Son brothers, challenged China's proclamation. With an army of 100,000 soldiers and 100 elephants, Nguyen Hue attacked Thang Long at night and routed the Chinese army. The Le emperor and the Chinese army retreated into Chinese territory. Nguyen Hue used his military victory to open up negotiations with China. He agreed to pay tribute to China if it would recognize his rule in Vietnam.

With Chinese agreement, Nguyen Hue declared the founding of the Tay Son dynasty (1788–1802). He established its capital near modern-day Hue so that his rule would encompass both North and South Vietnam. Nguyen Hue, who changed his name to Quang Trung, reorganized the government by placing the reigns of power into the hands of military generals rather than the scholars. He ordered that the official court language be Vietnamese rather than Chinese. To stimulate the war-ravaged economy, he encouraged foreign trade and ordered that taxes on local products be reduced. Landless farmers were given fallow land to cultivate.

Despite Quang Trung's attempts to unify and stabilize Vietnam, the Tay Son dynasty lasted only fourteen years. One reason for the brief Tay Son rule was that a scramble for power divided the court following its first emperor's death. Yet, its greatest failure was that it allowed the escape of Nguyen Anh, the previously-mentioned nephew of the last Nguyen lord. This young man proved to be the undoing of the Tay Son house, and the founder of Vietnam's last dynasty.

The Nguyen Dynasty
(1802–1954)

Nguyen Anh (1761–1820)

When the Tay Son soldiers routed the Nguyen army at Saigon in 1778, the Nguyen militia fled into the swamps of the Mekong Delta. The Tay Son generals ordered the execution of all the Nguyen lords and their immediate families, and Nguyen Anh was the only immediate member of the Nguyen ruling house to escape. Though he was only sixteen years of age, he had sufficient authority and charisma to rally the fleeing Nguyen forces. Under his leadership, Nguyen soldiers regrouped and retook Saigon. For several years control of the Saigon citadel changed hands. During 1783 the Tay Son forces overwhelmed the Nguyen army, and Nguyen Anh and his army sought refuge at Phu Quoc, an island in the Siam Gulf. His decision to take refuge on this island would change the course of world history.

Pierre Joseph Pigneau de Behaine (1744–1798)

Phu Quoc also housed a Roman Catholic seminary. At the time the school consisted of just a few huts and about forty students. The principle teacher at the academy was the French priest, Pierre Joseph Pigneau de Behaine. The eldest of nineteen children, Pigneau was raised in humble circumstances in the home of a tanner. He entered the ministry against his father's wishes and, in 1766, he was assigned to the Siam Gulf seminary as a member of the French Society of Foreign Missions. Upon arriving at the seminary, he found that the tropical heat caused chronic disease for the Europeans on the island. He also was taken aback by the numerous local civil wars. Naïve concerning these affairs, Pigneau provided aid to a Thai prince on the run. The prince's enemies arrived on the island and promptly put Pigneau in an eighty-pound wood and iron frame. He was released after three months, only to be the victim of a Cambodian invasion. Several of the seminary students were killed and Pigneau escaped to Malacca—the town at the tip of the Malay Peninsula. From there Pigneau made his way to the east coast of India, where the French had established the town of Pondicherry as a colony. Despite receiving the bishopric of a Middle Eastern city, Pigneau's heart was in Asia and, in 1775, he returned to Phu Quoc and revived the struggling seminary.

Fleeing for his life, Nguyen Anh, encountered Pigneau in 1783. A warm friendship quickly developed between the two men. In the course of their interaction, it became clear that both men needed each other. Pigneau wanted France to enjoy a special position in Vietnam, while Nguyen Anh needed outside aid to overthrow the Tay Son kings. An agreement was struck between the two. Pigneau would leave Phu Quoc and return with a French force that would be at Nguyen Anh's disposal. For his part, Nguyen Anh promised that he would cede the island of Poulo Condore and portions of the strategic Da Nang port to the French. As a proof of his sincerity, Nguyen Anh insisted that his five-year-old son, Prince Canh, accompany Pigneau on his overseas voyage.

Pigneau returned to Pondicherry, but he could not convince the local governor to release ships and military supplies for a Vietnamese expedition. Undeterred, the French cleric and his five-year-old companion traveled to France to appeal to King Louis XVI. Prince Canh's arrival at the French court was a subject of great interest. His particular hairstyle and language distinguished him from the young sons of the French monarch. Plagued by domestic troubles, Louis XVI was hesitant to commit any supplies to Nguyen Anh. However, he finally agreed to allow Pigneau to pick up several French ships and military supplies in Pondicherry. Overjoyed with the news, Pigneau quickly returned to the French colony only to find that the French king had sent secret orders to Pondicherry indicating that he did not wish any French material to be handed over to Nguyen Anh. Still undeterred, Pigneau independently raised funds for two ships and packed them with European mercenaries and military provisions. In 1789 the ships arrived in Vietnam and Pigneau returned Prince Canh, now a Christian, to his father.

The Reign of Gia Long (1802–1820)

Nguyen Anh used these supplies to regain control of southern Vietnam. With momentum on his side, he proceeded to send his army north and, in 1802, the Tay Son dynasty came to a quick end. Nguyen Anh declared the founding of the Nguyen dynasty (1802–1954). Vietnamese emperors usually changed their names when they began to rule, and Nguyen chose the symbolic name Gia Long. Gia Dinh (Saigon) was the major city in the South, while Thang Long (Hanoi) was the ancient capital in northern

Vietnam. By taking his name from these two cities, Gia Long made known his intent to rule a united Vietnam. He chose Hue in Central Vietnam as his capital to further demonstrate that he wanted all the Vietnamese to experience his benevolence. He sent tribute to China and had his ambassadors explain to the Qing court that heaven had placed him on the throne in a southern state that he intended to call Nam Viet. The Chinese recalled that the ancient Nam Viet had caused China a host of problems, so they sent messages to Gia Long that they would recognize him as the emperor of Viet Nam.

When Gia Long began his reign, he set out to make the Vietnam court a mirror image of the Chinese court. More than any of Vietnam's former rulers, the first Nguyen emperor insisted that Vietnam's worldview conform to Confucianism. The bureaucracy was filled with Vietnamese scholars who knew the Confucian classics. Court memorials were written with Chinese characters, and trade was discouraged. Like Qing China, Vietnam began to turn in on itself. The rights of women were repealed and ordinary farmers were forced to provide the government with sixty days of free labor every year.

Gia Long remained thankful to Pigneau for his aid and demonstrated his gratitude by giving the French priest an elaborate funeral. Despite his thankfulness, however, Gia Long never forgave Pigneau for converting his eldest son, Prince Canh, to Christianity. Moreover, Gia Long distrusted all forms of religion, and trained his other sons to rest on Confucian ideals rather than metaphysical beliefs.

A wonderful opportunity lay before Gia Long. Vietnam was united and its geographical boundaries extended beyond any previous measurements. China recognized its southern autonomous neighbor, and European states also acknowledged

Main gate to the imperial palace in Hue. Like the Chinese emperors, the Nguyen leaders lived in a city that was not accessible to the general public.

Gia Long's new state. Yet, for all these opportunities, Gia Long did not recognize that he could not maintain the status quo with regard to foreign countries. His narrow view of the world eventually resulted in Vietnam's downfall.

One can hardly blame the Nguyen emperor for failing to see the dramatic changes that the nineteenth century would bring not only to Asia but also to the world. China's prolonged political, economic, and social dominance over East and Southeast Asia created the mistaken idea among Asians that China was the Middle Kingdom around which the world would continue to revolve. Moreover, Gia Long and his constituents rested in the fact that since China was friendly toward them, all was calm on the international front. But the world was changing.

Economic and technological revolutions were transforming European countries, and these changes would eventually shift the balance of power away from the Middle Kingdom to the more technologically sophisticated European states. Gia Long's mistrust of Catholicism and his domestic-centered Confucian worldview meant that Vietnam avoided interaction with the European states that were rapidly growing in military strength.

Minh Mang (r.1820–1841)

As Gia Long's life came to an end, the most important decision for the future of Vietnam was the choice of his successor. Prince Canh was the emperor's oldest son, but he had died in 1801. It would have been natural for Gia Long to appoint Prince Canh's oldest son to be the Nguyen dynasty's second emperor. However, because of Prince Canh's former associations with the French, not to mention his conversion to Christianity, Gia Long chose Minh Mang because he knew this son embraced the isolation policy upon which the Nguyen dynasty was founded. The son of a concubine, Minh Mang was also his father's choice because Vietnam needed a mature leader to handle the numerous crises that plagued the country. Gia Long's domestic policies had created discontent among the farmers and over 105 rural uprisings took place between 1802 and 1820.

Minh Mang lived up to his father's expectations. He reorganized the empire into thirty-one provinces and placed competent scholars as governors of these districts. To improve Vietnam's economic situation he ordered that irrigation canals be repaired, fallow land be cultivated, and the empire's road system be extended. Even more anti-Christian than his father, Minh Mang outlawed the practice of this religion in Vietnam. He made it illegal for any foreign priest to set foot in Vietnam. Despite his anti-Christian laws, Minh Mang promoted trade with foreign countries and incorporated portions of Cambodia into the Nguyen empire.

The European population in Vietnam grew throughout the rule of the second Nguyen emperor. In particular, the French discovered that Vietnam was one of the remaining Southeast Asian countries that was not already dominated by the British, Dutch, or Spanish. Unfortunately for Minh Mang, the increased French population in Vietnam meant that France took a much keener interest in the domestic and foreign policies of this Asian state. Even though the anti-Christian laws in Vietnam were not strictly enforced, the Catholic Church in France denounced the Vietnamese emperor for his anti-Christian edicts. In the wake of the debacle of the French Revolution (1789) and the Napoleonic Wars (1804–1415), there was a resurgence of respect for the Catholic Church in France at the very time that Minh Mang was declaring his opposition to the Catholic religion. The popular press in France condemned Vietnam's anti-modern, anti-Christian policies.

Because the French population continued to grow in Vietnam, Minh Mang sent ambassadors to France to negotiate an agreement between the two countries. This was an early opportunity for France and Vietnam to work through their differences and establish a foundation for future relations. It did not happen. Under pressure from Church leaders and determined to display their unhappiness with Minh Mang, French politicians refused to meet with the Vietnamese delegates. Implications of this lost opportunity would have tragic consequences in the twentieth century.

French Pressure in Vietnam

Minh Mang passed away in 1841. His eldest son, Thieu Tri (r. 1841–1847), was subsequently enthroned as the Nguyen dynasty's third emperor. Thieu Tri's ascension to the throne coincided with an intensified interest in Vietnam on the part of France.

Around the time of Minh Mang's death, the dark clouds of European encroachment produced a storm in Asia that shocked the region to its very foundations. The gale centered on Chinese-British relations. Throughout the eighteenth and early nineteenth centuries, the British bought enormous amounts of tea from the Chinese. This tea was then sent to England and its colonies. England placed a tax on the sale of this product, making it a major source of revenue for the British government. This system benefited all involved, but as time passed, the British grew tired of the laws that the Chinese placed on purchasing Chinese tea. In particular, the British were bothered that their dealings with the Chinese were limited to the southern port town of Canton. Also, the British requested that the Chinese buy British products to offset the trade imbalance. Silver is what China required in exchange for its tea, and the Middle Kingdom was not interested in purchasing any of Britain's new-fangled machines. Tired of sinking all its silver into the Chinese market, the British discovered that their colony in India was a prime location for growing opium. They then smuggled this product into China and, as millions of Chinese became addicted to this narcotic, the trade imbalance shifted toward the British. In exchange for the opium, British merchants regularly received both tea and silver.

In an effort to halt opium's damaging economic and moral effects on China, the Qing emperor confiscated the British stock of this product in Canton. Britain responded by declaring war on China. For the few Vietnamese and other Asians who learned about this war, it was almost comical to believe that a small island-nation in the Atlantic Ocean would dare to provoke China. However, as Thieu Tri took power in Vietnam in 1841, he learned that this little European country had soundly defeated China. Moreover, they had forced the Asian nation to cede portions of its territory to England, to pay an enormous amount in reparations, and to open five ports on its eastern seaboard to international trade.

France intended to take advantage of the new opportunities for trade in Asia. Following the Opium War, the French stationed a permanent naval squadron in the South China Sea. The Vietnamese were cautiously optimistic that they would not fall into the same trap as China. However, behind this optimism was still a Confucian ideology that created a bureaucracy in which the emperor lived in a forbidden city within the confines of Hue. He was removed from the people, and he maintained a policy that kept Vietnam isolated from interaction with the West. He may have wanted to learn technology from the West, but he did not want Western influence in his empire.

For its part, France was emboldened by the events in China. In 1843 the French navy received tacit approval to intervene in Vietnam to recover imprisoned missionaries. The navy used this carte blanche order to bully its way into Vietnam's internal affairs. One example of its action is seen in the port of Tourane (Da Nang). In 1847 two French warships bombarded the Da Nang shoreline, killing approximately 10,000 Vietnamese on its banks, and destroying five Vietnamese ships. Their justification for this action was to gain the release of a priest who had actually been set free several weeks before. Thieu Tri vocally railed against the French, but there was little he could do. He died within a few weeks of this incident.

Upon Thieu Tri's death, Vietnam was at the edge of disaster. European nations were sinking their claws into lands throughout Asia. In the West capitalism had replaced state-controlled economic systems, and the Industrial Revolution produced entrepreneurs seeking raw materials and substantial markets. Asia had both and these various Asian states were the targets of both the industrial capitalists and Western governments bent on expanding their empires.

Tu Duc (r. 1847–1883)

To withstand the onslaught of Western imperialism, Vietnam needed a strong emperor. The rightful heir to Thieu Tri's throne was Hong Bao—his charismatic eldest son. Court intrigue placed Hong Bao's younger brother, Tu Duc, on the throne instead. This political manipulation was a tragic turn of events for Vietnam. Tu Duc was sickly, pessimistic, and fatalistic. He was not popular among the populace and he knew it. He was constantly fearful that his older brother would stage a coup against him.

The dreaded coup did occur in the mid-1850s, but Tu Duc's allies were able to defeat his political rivals and Tu Duc maintained his position as emperor. Given what occurred following the coup, one might wonder if Vietnam's fate would have been better off if Tu Duc's older brother had prevailed in the civil strife.

An early feature of Tu Duc's rule was a more active persecution of Christians in Vietnam. Unlike his predecessors, Tu Duc made sure that that the anti-Christian laws were vigorously enforced. All Vietnamese Christians were ordered to have their cheeks branded with the characters "ta dao," or infidel. Foreign priests were drowned, and Vietnamese priests were sawed in half. Unpopular at home, Tu Duc was now internationally detested.

In France pressure was placed on Louis Napoleon to take military action against the Vietnamese emperor both by his staunchly Catholic Spanish wife, Eugenia, and France's naval officials and merchants. In response to these pressures, Napoleon III authorized military incursions in Vietnam. In 1858 French troops captured the strategic port of Da Nang and, in the following year, they occupied Saigon.

All in all, the results of France's initial battles in Vietnam were a great disappointment for the European state. The French believed that the Catholic Vietnamese communities would rise

Mandarin (scholar) of Emperor Tu Duc in full regalia.

French Indochina

up and join the invading forces, but this did not take place. Once the French troops landed in Vietnam, they found that they could not establish peace in the area. The Vietnamese militia constantly harassed the French troops. Worse yet, more French troops perished from the tropical diseases such as cholera and typhoid than from engagements with Vietnamese freedom fighters. Beset by these difficulties, the French withdrew from Da Nang. They continued to tentatively occupy small areas of Saigon.

The Unequal Treaties

Determined to press its claim on Vietnam, France sent an expedition of seventy ships and 3,500 men to reinforce its troops in Saigon during 1861. This act was correctly interpreted by the Vietnamese as the beginning of France's colonizing adventures in Vietnam. Bloody battles took place for the city of Saigon. Like the earlier conflict between the Chinese and the British, France's superior weapons overcame the fact that they were outnumbered by Vietnamese soldiers. In a somewhat surprising move, Emperor Tu Duc quickly sued for peace.

The terms that France received in the 1862 Treaty of Saigon were very generous: Saigon and its three neighboring provinces were ceded to France; foreign merchants were given free access to three Vietnamese ports; missionary activity was legalized throughout Vietnam; French warships were given free passage up the Mekong River; and the Vietnamese court paid France a handsome indemnity for losing the war.

There were reasons that Tu Duc signed this unequal treaty with the French. First, the southern portion of Vietnam was at the periphery of his court's concern. In many ways this region was still viewed as the frontier. A telling statistic is that of the

1,024,338 male tax payers in the official 1847 census, only 165,598 lived in the southern provinces. Tu Duc concluded that there was little to lose in giving this sparsely populated area to the French. In addition, there was a domestic crisis brewing in the North. Christian-led rebels were threatening the peace of Thang Long (Hanoi), and Tu Duc wanted his army to concentrate on crushing this rebellion.

The emperor's gamble paid off handsomely. By moving his troops North, the Nguyen court successfully crushed the rebels. Thousands of Vietnamese Christians were killed in these battles, but the French did not loudly protest this massacre because they had Tu Duc to thank for their position in the South.

Following his victory in the North, the Vietnamese court renegotiated its treaty with France. Tu Duc orchestrated a deal whereby the French would return the three southern provinces to the Vietnamese court. In exchange, the Vietnamese court agreed that France could claim a protectorate of Cochinchina—the six provinces that made up Vietnam's southern region. A protectorate status meant that France would control the region's foreign relations, domestic affairs, and its economy.

France agreed to this deal and quickly moved up the Mekong River into Cambodia. By 1863 the Cambodian monarch was also forced to recognize that his country was a protectorate of the French. Thailand, Cambodia's western neighbor, protested France's growing control of Vietnam and Cambodia. France appeased the Thai monarch by forcing Cambodia to relinquish two of its western provinces to Thailand.

While France was happy to control Cochinchina and Cambodia, it was not yet content. Merchants and military personnel believed that the real value of Vietnam was its northern areas. Many French viewed Vietnam merely as a stepping-stone to increased trade with and exploitation of China. With this in mind, the French organized an expedition to determine whether a waterway passage connected China and Vietnam via the Mekong River.

Lieutenant Francis Garnier was assigned to this two-year mission that began in June 1866. In 1873 Garnier published a two-volume study, *Voyage d'Exploration,* in which he presented an outline of his exploration of northern Vietnam and southern China. He concluded that it was impossible for a boat to reach China via the Mekong River. However, he wrote that the Red River was the perfect passageway from China's southern province of Yunan to the Vietnamese port of Haiphong. More importantly, he claimed that France was falling behind times in its inability to garner colonies. The message was quite clear: France should incorporate all of Vietnam into its empire.

Responding to this message, French merchants and soldiers flocked to the northern portion of Vietnam, also known as Tonkin. In 1873 Emperor Tu Duc responded to the increased French presence in the North by once again renegotiating the Saigon Treaty. In the new agreement, Tu Duc agreed that the France would enjoy complete sovereignty, rather than a protectorate status, in Cochinchina. He also agreed to allow the French to trade up and down the Red River. Anxious to press these gains, Garnier set out to remove any obstructions that might impede trade from the Vietnamese coast to Hanoi. The mood of Vietnamese and Chinese merchants was expressed in their reaction to Garnier. Refusing to allow him to pass, Chinese mercenaries and anti-French Vietnamese soldiers attacked and killed Garnier. They removed his head and paraded it through the surrounding villages.

The Vietnam History Museum in Hanoi was once the archaeological research institution of the French School of the Far East.

Garnier's death set back French plans to control the Tonkin area, but only temporarily. Nine years later, France commissioned Henri Rivierre and 600 troops to establish order in Tonkin. Rivierre soon met the same fate as Garnier. France responded with a massive show of force, attacking Hue in 1883. The ailing Emperor Tu Duc died hearing the blasts of French canon around his capital. Probably sterile, Tu Duc did not have children. Debate raged at court as to the choice of a successor, as well as how to deal with the French.

Within a year of Tu Duc's death, three emperors were enthroned and deposed, further destabilizing the shaky imperial court. Meanwhile, France pressed its claims on a Vietnamese court that was in chaos. The court was forced to sign a treaty in August 1883, one month after Tu Duc's death, wherein the Vietnamese recognized a French protectorate over Tonkin and Annam (central Vietnam), while Cochinchina remained a part of the French empire. France would assume Vietnam's foreign relations, and the Vietnamese emperor would have limited power. One year later, in June 1884, the scholar officials recognized this humiliating situation and signed the Treaty of Protectorate, agreeing to French suzerainty over their lands. Once again Vietnam was entirely in the hands of a foreign nation. Only this time it was not with a contiguous northern neighbor, but with a nation across several oceans.

France had numerous reasons for wanting to control Vietnam. Religious, economic, and military advisors each had their justifications for the French intrusion into Asia. In France's academies and journals, the primary justification for ruling Vietnam was termed *Mission Civilasatrice,* or the mission to civilize. Herbert Spencer's (1820–1903) theories of social evolution were the rage of intellectual Europe. These theories espoused that Western society represented the most advanced civilization, thus it was the West's responsibility to spread its advancements to the rest of humanity. Western physicians, teachers, and social workers gave up lives of relative comfort to spread what they believed was their advanced civilization to remote regions of the world. In Vietnam, the French began the process of "civilizing" the indigenous peoples by organizing the region. In 1887 the French created the Indochinese Union (ICU), which encompassed Cochinchina as a colony, and Annam, Tonkin, and Cambodia as French protectorates. Laos was added to the ICU as a protectorate in 1893.

Recognizing that it would be best to work through existing institutions, the French did not depose the Nguyen emperors but kept them as puppets. In Tonkin and Annam, the French continued to use successful candidates of the Confucian civil exam to fill the lower levels in the bureaucracy. French officials micromanaged the ICU, with Vietnamese civil servants receiving only the lower positions in the government. A prerequisite for Vietnamese employment in the ICU was proof of loyalty to France.

An early governor-general of the ICU was Paul Doumer (1897–1902). He fashioned policies that would shape Vietnam for the first half of the twentieth century. Doumer insisted that the populace of the ICU should pay all of France's expenses in the region, including the handsome salaries of more than 5,000 French ICU officials. To this end a state monopoly was placed on the sale and taxation of salt, alcohol, and opium.

To encourage industry in Vietnam, large tracts of land were sold to French *colons* (colonial settlers). The Mekong Delta became the center for large French-owned rubber plantations. A few elite Vietnamese and Chinese families also bought land and functioned within the ICU economic parameters. However, by 1920, ninety percent of the rubber plantations in Vietnam were owned by French *colons*.

ICU officials also sought to increase their funds by forcing the Vietnamese to export rice—something that had been forbidden by most Vietnamese emperors. Apart from the taxes that were placed on the Vietnamese, ICU officials demanded that Vietnamese men donate a certain amount of their time to government projects. All of these policies had a devastating effect on the Vietnamese farmer. By 1930, fifty-seven percent of the rural population in Cochinchina was landless, along with almost two million northern farmers.

During the first decades of the ICU, there were many revolts against the harsh French rule. However, most of these uprisings were localized. (The idea of nationalism still a generation away.) Some of the revolts did center on the desire to restore

Ham Nghi.

the emperor's prestige. In 1885, for example, Ton That Thuyet, the regent for twelve-year-old Emperor Ham Nghi, removed the royal family from Hue and ordered that the French advisor in Hanoi be thrown out of Tonkin. Known in history as the can vuoun (aid the king), this revolt earned the support of a great number of Vietnamese. However, the power of the French was demonstrated in November 1888, when they captured Emperor Ham Nghi. He was exiled to Algeria for the remainder of his life, and died in 1947.

France was initially successful in governing the ICU. They made it clear that Vietnam was to be three states: Tonkin, Annam, and Cochinchina. They did not refer to Vietnam's inhabitants as Vietnamese, a semantic ploy meant to emphasize the disunity of the region. As a generation of Vietnamese grew up under French rule, however, they began nationalist movements based on new ideologies and the staggering changes around the world, and in Asia particularly.

Vietnamese Nationalism

A primary factor for the Vietnamese independence movements was the strict rule that France placed on the ICU. It was illegal for Vietnamese to travel outside their villages unless they had special papers from the government; it was illegal to publish any material without French permission; and the Vietnamese had to receive French permission to have any type of public or private assembly meeting. Though the harsh rule of France in Vietnam is the primary reason that the Vietnamese rebelled, it was not the sole one. Indeed, the subject of early Vietnamese nationalist movements is complex. It is made clearer by focusing on two of its principle leaders, and their relationships with Vietnam's two neighboring countries: Japan and China.

Phan Boi Chau (1867–1940)

Phan Boi Chau was born into a northern Vietnamese family of scholars. He was working his way up the civil service ladder, when he became disillusioned by the unfair and racist French policies. In 1903 he located Cuong De, a descendent of Gia

Suspected anti–French prisoners.

Long, and announced to his colleagues that he intended to install him as the rightful emperor of Vietnam. Phan Boi Chau believed his restoration movement would be more effective if it were in a foreign land where the French could not persecute its followers. Accordingly, Phan Boi Chau brought Cuong De to Japan, where they were free to publish and speak out against the French occupation of their country.

In 1906 Japan was experiencing unprecedented international prestige. In less than half a century, it had emerged from a semi-feudal state to a modern nation that had defeated China in 1895 and imperial Russia in 1905. Japan was the model example of a "first-class nation." Phan Boi Chau sought out the small Vietnamese community in Japan. Finding more than 100 Vietnamese students in Japan, he organized the Viet Nam Cong Hien Hoi (Vietnam Public Offering Society). The name of his new organization was significant because the designation for the land they wished to recover was not Tonkin, Annam, or Cochinchina. For the emerging nationalists, the geographical boundaries that the ICU placed on Vietnam were artificial and had to be removed.

The political freedom that Phan Boi Chau thought he had in Japan disappeared in 1908, when French authorities persuaded the Japanese to deport this rabble-rouser. He fled to southern China and found himself inspired by the Chinese nationalist leader, Dr. Sun Yat-sen. With the imperial system crumbling in China, Dr. Sun Yat-sen preached that the country should move toward a socialist democracy based on nationalism. Phan Boi Chau caught this vision and restructured his movement so that the ultimate goal for Vietnam became the construction of a democracy based on nationalism. He established the Modernization Society in 1912, with the express purpose of expelling the French from Vietnam.

Dr. Sun Yat–sen, whose principles of nationalism attracted Vietnam's anti–colonial nationalists.

Vietnamese imprisoned following a failed revolt against the French in 1907.

Unhappy with the slow progress of this movement, Phan Boi Chau ordered that acts of terrorism be carried out against ICU French officials. He believed that when expatriate Vietnamese heard about these attacks, they would be willing to contribute money to the Modernization Society. It did not happen. Instead the French cracked down even more on forms of Vietnamese nationalist sentiment. French paranoia in the ICU grew to the point that, in 1916, they exiled another Nguyen emperor, Duy Tran (r. 1907–1916), to Reunion Island in the Indian Ocean. In 1925 Phan Boi Chau was captured by French agents in the international section of Shanghai, brought to Vietnam, and placed under house arrest until his death in 1940.

Phan Chu Trinh (1872–1926)

Phan Chu Trinh, from an elite military family, was the second major figure in Vietnam's nationalist movement. Like others of his generation, he was influenced by the writings of Rosseau and Montisque, which were available in Chinese translations. The spread of new ideas in the Tonkin area was also facilitated by the increased use of *quoc ngu*, the romanized form of Vietnamese writing.

From the outset, Phan Chu Trinh differed from Phan Boi Chau in that he did not think that the answer for Vietnam lay in the restoration of the Nguyen emperor or even an abrupt French withdrawal. Rather, Phan Chu Trinh believed that the Vietnamese should learn from the French and hold their colonial mother accountable for their stated goal to civilize Vietnam. ICU bureaucrats considered his writings subversive and imprisoned him in 1908. He was later exiled to France, but received permission to return to his homeland in 1925. One year later, his funeral turned into a demonstration against the French, evidence that a nationalistic fervor had erupted in Vietnam.

Cochinchina and Nationalism

Most of the early nationalist leaders were from the Tonkin and Annam areas. Historically this region was home to the ancient capital of Thang Long and the Nguyen dynasty's capital at Hue. On the other hand, Cochinchina was a recent addition to Vietnam's territory; it was sparsely populated; it was a colony—not a protectorate—of France; and there was a large percentage of ethnic minorities in this southern section. Furthermore, manufacturing in the area was limited to cement and textiles for domestic use, and the economy was directed by the rich, for the rich.

As noted earlier, French colonizers and a few Vietnamese elite families had purchased large portions of Cochinchina's land. The governing arm of the French in the colony was the Colonial Council of Cochinchina (CCC), which included sixteen French and six Vietnamese members. Bui Quang Chieu, a French-trained engineer who was also part of the Vietnamese landed elite in Cochinchina, argued that France should place more Vietnamese representatives on the CCC. To bolster his case he founded the Constitutional Party in 1917.

This group requested that France institute a modernized bureaucracy in Cochinchina; reform the naturalization law, which made it difficult for Vietnamese to gain French citizenship; and curtail the Chinese merchants' hold on Cochinchina's economy. Like the British in Malaya, the French catered to the Chinese population when it came to economic interests because the Chinese were less likely to fuss about independence. Furthermore, the overseas Chinese had a network of economic allies that allowed them to flourish wherever they lived. The council took some of these requests under advisement and raised the number of Vietnamese representatives on the council from six to ten.

Bui Quang Chieu chose the right historical moment to found the Constitutional Party. During 1917 France was locked in a life-and-death struggle in Europe. World War I so occupied France's attention that it needed Vietnamese bureaucrats to fill positions throughout the ICU. Moreover, more than 100,000 Vietnamese were shipped to France to assist in the war effort. An unintended consequence of this recruitment was that the Vietnamese discovered that they were treated with greater respect in France, by French citizens, than they were in Vietnam by French officials. More than that, they observed that France itself had numerous economic, social, and political difficulties. For many Vietnamese, these observations demythologized the grandeur and awe they had previously given their colonial mother. They returned to Vietnam with a confidence that was rooted in their European experience.

It is said that the blood of the early Christian martyrs was the seed of a Church that would eventually conquer Rome itself. Similarly, French intimidation and persecution of Vietnam's early nationalist leaders only increased Vietnamese resistance to foreign rule. As World War I concluded, Vietnamese leaders continued to search for a model they could use to bring freedom and unity to their country. Because of its long history with China, it was somewhat natural for Vietnam to look to its northern neighbor for guidance.

By the late 1920s, China was divided in its race for modernity and democracy. China's main political party during this period was the Nationalist Party or Kuomintang (KMT), led by Dr. Sun Yat-sen. He died in 1925, however, and the KMT's mantle of leadership fell to General Chiang Kai-shek. The Nationalist pattern for modernizing China was countered by the ideology of the Chinese Communist Party (CCP). Following the lead of the Soviet Union, the Chinese Communists lobbied for a fundamental shift in China's economy and social structure. The KMT and CCP leadership were sharply divided, and by 1928 these two parties were at war with each other.

Nguyen Thai Hoc and the VNQDD

In Vietnam, two nationalist figures emerged during this era. The first leader, Nguyen Thai Hoc, incorporated the KMT model for Vietnam. He received aid and advice from China's Nationalist Party. The second gentleman gravitated to the CCP model. He traveled to Paris and the Soviet Union before settling down to work with the Chinese Communists. Biding his time until Vietnam was ripe for a communist revolution, he studied and wrote about Marxist doctrine as it fit the Vietnamese experience. This person is known as Ho Chi Minh.

Born to a peasant family in the Red River Delta, Nguyen Thai Hoc (1904–1930) studied commerce and education in Hanoi. At first he advocated moderate political reform. However, as his letters to the French authorities were ignored, Nguyen Thai Hoc's vision for Vietnam took a radical turn. He based his independence movement on the Chinese KMT model. Using a Hanoi bookstore as a front for his illegal political activities, Nguyen Thai Hoc founded the Viet Nam Quoc Dan Dang (VNQDD), the Vietnamese Nationalist Party, in the fall of 1927.

Despite the amount of time and energy VNQDD leadership spent on bolstering its membership, it was for the most part made up of northern intellectuals and merchants. On February 9, 1929, in an attempt to attract southern support, the VNQDD assassinated René Bazin, the French official who was known for his cruel tactics in recruiting laborers for southern plantations. Unfortunately, this act did not produce southern support or the grassroots uprising that the VNQDD had hoped. It did expose the radical nature of the VNQDD, however, and French detectives promptly arrested hundreds of suspected VNQDD sympathizers.

In response to this setback, Nguyen Thai Hoc regrouped the scattered VNQDD members and ordered an all-out revolution against the French on February 10, 1930. The French quickly squashed this revolt, capturing and guillotining numerous VNQDD leaders, including Nguyen Thai Hoc. While there remained a VNQDD remnant, the Vietnamese Nationalist Party never fully recovered from its ill-timed uprising. The dwindling influence of the VNQDD created a revolutionary vacuum that the Vietnamese Communists would fill.

Ho Chi Minh and the Vietnamese Communist Party

Of all the regions in the ICU, the district that the French had the most trouble with was the central Vietnamese province of Nghe An. The province is known for unfertile topsoil that has very little depth. Bordering the Tonkin Gulf, annual floods often ravaged the small number of crops that the farmers grew. It was in Nghe An, in May 1890, that a boy was born to a poor family. He

French guillotine in Hanoi's Hoa Lo Prison. It is a reminder that many Vietnamese, including Nguyen Thai Hoc, lost their lives fighting the French.

was named Nguyen Sin Cung but, at the age of eleven, his name was changed to Nguyen Tat Thanh (He who will succeed). The new name was indicative of the boy's propensities. From an early age Thanh appeared to have a gift for learning. In this he followed his father who was the first man from the village to pass the highest civil service exam.

Thanh was sent to Hue, where he studied at the prestigious National Academy. Following his graduation, Thanh tried his hand at teaching. Ambition pushed him south, where he took a job as a cook's assistant on a French ship in 1911. This allowed him to travel the globe, and he visited portions of Asia, Africa, the United States, and Europe. He stayed in London for a short time, and eventually settled in Paris where he took the name Nguyen Ai Quoc (Nguyen the patriot). While in Paris he began to study the writings of Karl Marx and Vladimir Lenin, as well as the philosophy of U.S. President Woodrow Wilson.

Following World War I, President Wilson traveled to the Versailles Peace Conference outside of Paris. The American leader argued in his Fourteen Point Program that nations should enjoy self-determination. Nguyen Ai Quoc attempted to meet with President Wilson to present a case for Vietnamese independence. This meeting did not take place, however, and the Versailles Peace Conference did nothing to alleviate the ugly exploitation that accompanied imperialism.

In the midst of his disappointment at the outcome of the Versailles Conference, Nguyen Ai Quoc read Lenin's 1920 "Thesis on the National and Colonial Questions." That same year, he became a founding member of the French Communist Party (FCP). In 1923, Nguyen Ai Quoc traveled to Moscow to participate in the Fifth International Communist (Comintern) Congress. While at the conference, he attracted the attention of

Russian and Chinese leaders. He traveled to China and then to Russia, where he continued his intense study of Marxism.

Meanwhile, numerous communist organizations appeared throughout Vietnam. These groups competed against each other, so the Comintern sent Nguyen Ai Quoc to Vietnam in 1930 in order to unite the disparate groups. At a meeting in Hong Kong, he and the other Vietnamese communist factions established the Indochina Communist Party (ICP). A Central Committee was formed and was comprised of nine members: three from Tonkin, two from Annam, two from Cochinchina, and two from the Vietnamese community in China. The transcending stated goals of the ICP were to remove France from Indochina and to create a government where the exploitation of people would cease.

The ICP was born into a troubled world. World markets were devastated by the global depression, and Vietnam was not spared economic hardship. French investors withdrew from Vietnam; the world market price for rice was slashed in half; and rubber exports in 1930 brought in only one-fourth what they had in 1928. The rich ensured that they survived the economic storm, while the farmers had to bring in the same amount of annual tax. This system meant farmers had to produce double the amount of rice they had prior to the depression just to pay their taxes and debts. Urban centers experienced upheaval as the incidents of strikes increased from seven in 1927 to ninety-eight just two years later.

The increased economic hardship of the poor provided an opportunity for communist agents to explain capitalist exploitation to Vietnam's starving peasants. Communist representatives infiltrated Nguyen Ai Quoc's home province of Nghe An and created small communist communities that were known as

Ho Chi Minh at a Socialist Party Conference in France in December 1920.

soviets. In these communist districts, taxes were reduced and food was distributed to the weak as well as the strong. Positive changes in Nghe An created momentum that quickly spread to neighboring provinces.

French officials sensed the danger of losing control in Vietnam. They responded to the communist gains by sending French Foreign Legion soldiers to break up the soviets while using airplanes to bomb civilian targets. Over 1,000 ICP suspects were arrested and sent to prison. Nguyen Ai Quoc, still in Hong Kong, was also arrested. He spent two years in prison, and upon his release, fled to Russia where he recuperated. While there, he continued to write articles that were secretly distributed throughout Vietnam. Though most Vietnamese had never seen Nguyen Ai Quoc (he had not been in Vietnam for almost twenty-five years), his reputation as a revolutionary leader continued to grow.

World War II and Vietnam

World War II was truly global in scope. Events in one part of the world had a profound effect on other parts. This was particularly true for France and Vietnam. Both countries had neighbors that coveted their territories, and Germany's invasion of France had a profound effect on Vietnam. The Germans established a pro-German Vichy Government, which also controlled Indochina. Meanwhile, on the Asian continent, Japan was entrenched in a military campaign against China that had erupted two years before the outbreak of war in Europe. Japanese advisors, particularly naval officers, believed that Japan needed to occupy portions of Southeast Asia. Japan's hope was that it would eventually create a Greater East Asian Co-Prosperity Sphere, wherein Asia's economy would be centered in Japan. Southeast Asia held the promise of markets and raw materials—especially oil. In 1940 Japan was receiving eighty-five percent of its oil from the United States.

Japan's first step into Southeast Asia lay through Tonkin, or northern Vietnam. On September 23, 1940, just weeks after the establishment of the Vichy Government, Japan invaded Tonkin and stationed troops in Hanoi. With very few options, the Vichy government acquiesced to Japan's desire to occupy Tonkin. However, the United States protested Japan's aggressions against Vietnam and placed a scrap metal embargo on Japan.

The Founding of the Vietminh

Nguyen Ai Quoc, now known as Ho Chi Minh (he who enlightens), rightly perceived that this might be an opportune time for the ICP to make headway in Vietnam. France was weakened by its war in Europe, and the United States seemed serious in its warnings to Japan. After being absent from Vietnam for thirty years, Ho returned to his country in February 1941 and took up residence in a cave at Pac Bo, near the China-Vietnam border. Several months later, the Eighth Plenum of the ICP convened and made decisions that would affect the history of Vietnam and its national struggle. It was agreed that national freedom took precedent over ideological or class struggle, and that the ICP would work with any organization that shared a vision of nationalism. Furthermore, the leaders agreed that guerilla warfare, urban and rural personnel, and non-conventional warfare would all be used to dislodge the French and Japanese from Vietnam. The League for the Independence of Vietnam (Viet Nam Doc Lap Dong Minh Hoi, Vietminh for short) was also established and commissioned to unite with all likeminded Vietnamese for national liberty. The Vietminh's ultimate goal was the removal of imperialist nations from Vietnam and the creation of a socialist republic.

The Japanese Occupation of Vietnam (1941–1945)

In July 1941 the Japanese expanded their Vietnamese base in Tonkin and occupied Annam and Cochinchina, unconcerned about United States' protests since they had signed a Tripartite Alliance with Germany and Italy.

There were two major implications of Japan's invasion of southern Vietnam. First, the United States responded to Japan's action by freezing all of Japan's assets in America and by placing an embargo on oil exportation to Japan. The second consequence of Japan's invasion was that Ho Chi Minh ordered the Vietminh to step up their attacks on the occupying Japanese army. Ho himself remained on the China-Vietnam border and, in 1942, the Vietminh received a setback when a Chinese Nationalist general captured and imprisoned him. He remained in captivity for two years. When he did gain his freedom in 1944, he immediately returned to northern Vietnam to lead the battle against the Japanese.

The Vietminh officials were forward looking. They understood that it was just a matter of time until Japan lost the war. Ho Chi Minh contacted members of America's Office of Strategic Services (OSS), the precursor to the Central Intelligence Agency (CIA). The Vietminh gave protection to U.S. pilots shot down by the Japanese, and, in early 1945, OSS personnel provided vital medical aid to a gravely ill Ho Chi Minh. At this same time, the desperate Japanese declared Vietnam's independence. They imprisoned the French officials, and recognized the Hue-based Nguyen emperor, Bao Dai, as the sovereign ruler of an independent Vietnam. Ho Chi Minh and his colleagues were not fooled. They knew that Emperor Bao Dai was a puppet of Japan. Furthermore, the Vietminh knew that should the Japanese lose the war, then France had lost its right to rule the Vietnamese.

Throughout the spring and summer of 1945, the Japanese struggled to keep peace in Vietnam. However, during these months, Japan's main focus was not on Southeast Asia. By May 1945, Germany had surrendered and U.S. troops were on the steps of Japanese territory. In July 1945 the Russian, British, and American leaders met at Potsdam, Germany to map out strategies following the war. While Vietnam was merely a side issue on the Potsdam agenda, it was discussed. The resolution was that the British would accept the Japanese capitulation south of the sixteenth parallel, and China's KMT Army would accept the Japanese surrender north of the sixteenth parallel. What was not fully disclosed at the conference was that the war was the impending use of nuclear weapons. The Allied powers at Potsdam also failed to recognize how powerful the Vietminh had become in Indochina.

In early August 1945, the Indochina Communist Party met for its Ninth Plenum. At the conference it was resolved that the time had arrived for a concentrated assault against the Japanese occupying force. The timing for the Vietminh's so-called August Revolution was perfect. Japanese policies in Vietnam had led to starvation and extreme poverty for millions of Vietnam's peasants. This harrowing economic situation was a result of Japan's insistence that the Japanese farmers pull out their rice crops and plant hemp for the war effort. The rice that was harvested was given to the Japanese, while millions of Vietnamese starved. August was also the month that the U.S. dropped two atomic bombs on Japan, bringing World War II to an abrupt end.

THE DEMOCRATIC REPUBLIC
OF VIETNAM (1945–1975)

The Founding of the DRV

Japan's surrender in Vietnam created a political vacuum. Since the Vietminh were in the midst of their August Revolution, their momentum propelled them into the political void. On September 2, 1945, Ho Chi Minh declared the founding of the Democratic Republic of Vietnam (DRV). It is instructive to note how he began this declaration:

> "All men are created equal. They are endowed by their Creator with certain inalienable rights; among these are Life, Liberty, and the pursuit of Happiness."
>
> This immortal statement was made in the Declaration of Independence of the United States of America in 1776. In a broader sense, this means: All the peoples on the earth are equal from birth, all the peoples have a right to live, to be happy and free.
>
> The Declaration of the French Revolution made in 1791 on the Rights of Man and the Citizen also states: "Also men are born free and with equal rights, and must always remain free and have equal rights."
>
> Those are undeniable truths.

Nevertheless, for more than eighty years, the French imperialists, abusing the standard of Liberty, Equality, and Fraternity, have violated our Fatherland and oppressed our fellow-citizens. They have acted contrary to the ideals of humanity and justice.

Ho Chi Minh's speech at the founding of the DRV added legitimacy to the Vietminh's successes. The Vietminh was strongest in northern Vietnam for numerous reasons. First, the headquarters of the Vietminh during World War II was on the China-Vietnam border. Second, Hanoi was the center of anti-French and anti-Japanese activity. The best opportunities for higher education were in Hanoi, and these schools produced leftist political students who identified with the ideology of the Vietminh. Finally, during World War II, the Vietminh were successful in establishing ties with Vietnam's northern rural communities. Following Ho's 1945 founding of the DRV, the Vietminh successfully replaced the colonial bureaucratic apparatus in Tonkin and Annam. At Hue, the capital city of Annam, Emperor Bao Dai turned over the reigns of power to the Vietminh. He then moved to Hanoi to serve as an advisor for the new government.

The Southern Resistance

In southern Vietnam, however, the people of Cochinchina resisted the encroaching Vietminh political system. Different groups carved out their spheres of influence in post-war Cochinchina. For example, Cao Dai and Hoa Hao were two religious organizations that wielded significant political and social control in Cochinchina immediately after World War II.

The Cao Dai "High Tower" religion was founded in 1919 by Ngo Van Chieu, a minor official of the French colonial government. Its founder reportedly received a message from a superior spirit that commanded him to bring all religions together to worship the one divine being. Ngo Van Chieu combined the doctrines of various faiths, including Buddhism, Confucianism, Islam, Daoism, and Christianity. Historical figures such as Napoleon Bonaparte, Sun Yat-sen, and Winston Churchhill were (and are) revered in this religion. During World War II, Cao Dai leaders cooperated with the Japanese occupying force. Following Japan's surrender, hundreds of thousands of Cao Dai followers looked forward to the return of the French. Since the headquarters of the Cao Dai religion was in the southern city of Tay Ninh, near the Cambodian border, most of its followers were the rural peasants of Cochinchina. They were wary of northerners, particularly the Vietminh, and the Cao Dai sect actively fought the communist intrusion into Cochinchina.

Hoa Hao was also a fast-growing religion in Cochinchina during World War II. Founded in 1939 by a young Buddhist mystic, Huynh Phu, the emphasis in this offshoot of Buddhism is simplicity. Hoa Hao leaders incorporated folk beliefs into the new religion's doctrines, and they called for social justice. This religion appealed to the rural population for two reasons. First, the syncretic approach of mixing in indigenous traditions and social programs was something with which the farmers could identify. Second, the prominence this religion placed on simplicity included a rejection of altars, temples, or any other hallowed trappings. This simplicity meant that Hoa Hao followers were not pressed to pay for costly sacred accessories. Like the Cao Dai believers, the Hoa Hao rebuffed the Vietminh's call for a national revolution. In 1947 the Vietminh assassinated Huynh

Phu, which drove the religion even further from the northern-based communist regime.

While these indigenous organizations made it difficult for the Vietminh to include Cochinchina into the DRV, the real problem was an outsider. General Douglas Gracey was the British general who led the Allied army into Cochinchina and accepted the Japanese surrender. Overextending his authority, Gracey proclaimed martial law in Cochinchina in an attempt to halt the fighting between the various factions. With a limited force of eighteen hundred troops at his disposal, Gracey released and armed fourteen hundred French troops. These soldiers spread throughout Saigon and brutally crushed the southern arm of the DRV government. Their rampage encouraged French civilians and members of the two religious sects to indiscriminately attack and loot any Vietnamese business that was suspected of supporting the DRV. General Gracey himself had to beg the French soldiers to moderate their campaign.

The Northern Invasion

While the DRV was struggling to survive in the South, a greater danger appeared from the North. Based on the Potsdam agreement, President Chiang Kai-shek unleashed the Chinese KMT Army on northern Vietnam. More than 200,000 KMT troops descended on Hanoi. Ho Chi Minh knew that the Vietminh were not in a position to fight this massive Chinese army, and he initially attempted to negotiate with the generals of the Chinese-occupying force. However, he quickly concluded that the Chinese were much more dangerous than the French and that the Chinese militia members that occupied

Hanoi were an undisciplined group. They stole everything that they could get their hands on, including doorknobs. Many of the soldiers brought their families with them, and the DRV feared that anti-communist Chiang Kai-shek would use the DRV ideology as a pretext for his army to remain in Hanoi. With very few options before him, Ho Chi Minh requested that the French return their pre-war forces to Tonkin.

The French obliged and the Chinese retreated north to fight their own civil war. Once in the northern capital, the French occupying force realized that the DRV was, for all intents and purposes, in control of northern and central Vietnam. Ho Chi Minh negotiated with the French and they came to this agreement in March 1946: the French would recognize the DRV as an independent state and would agree to a future plebiscite in Cochinchina; in return, the DRV agreed to be part of the proposed French Union (the new name for the French empire), and it would allow a small contingent of French soldiers in northern Vietnam.

A few months after this preliminary agreement, Ho traveled to France to negotiate the final details. It was one of the most disappointing moments of his life. When he arrived in France, he was pawned off to second-tier government officials. France insisted that Cochinchina remain a full-fledged colony and that the DRV permit French merchants and soldiers to hold special positions in the DRV-controlled areas. Ho Chi Minh tried everything he could to get the French to recognize that Cochinchina was part of Vietnam and that the Vietminh would not accept a divided Vietnam. Inflexible, the French Government told Ho Chi Minh to take or leave the agreement. On September 19, 1946, Ho signed the settlement and noted, "I've just signed my death warrant."

Ho Chi Minh was correct about the Vietminh outrage with this agreement. What he did not expect was how rudely many of the French citizens in Tonkin would treat the DRV officials. Many French soldiers gave lip service to the DRV control of northern Vietnam, while in practice they acted as though they were autonomous. French citizens in Hanoi continued to believe that the real power in the area was France, and they conducted business according to this assumption. An area particularly volatile for French-DRV relations was the port of Haiphong. A key harbor in the Tonkin Gulf, French business people used Haiphong for import and export transactions. This type of business was encouraged by the DRV, but, as with all countries, duty officers presided over incoming and outgoing commerce. French merchants took exception to this oversight and loudly protested the DRV inspectors' intrusion into their trade. In November 1946, barely two months after Ho Chi Minh had signed the agreement with France, French ships bombarded the port town of Haiphong. The next month French troops were sent to Hanoi to restore "order" to the region. The Vietminh declared that it was now at war with France. The First Indochina War had begun.

The First Indochina War (1946–1954)

Because of superior weaponry, the French quickly recaptured the urban areas in Vietnam following their attack on Haiphong. Yet, the People's Army of Vietnam believed that their tactics would eventually lead to a glorious victory. The military's confidence was based on the leadership ability of its general, Vo Nguyen Giap—a man with many talents and a tragic past.

Giap was from a peasant family and was drawn to the independence movement as a young man. In 1930 he joined the ICP and eventually received his law degree from the University of Hanoi. Following his graduation, he taught history at the Thang Long school in Hanoi, where he was particularly interested in great historical generals and battles. He married Nguyen Thi Minh Giang, the sister of Nguyen Thi Minh Khai who had been an earlier romantic interest and rumored wife of Ho Chi Minh. Giap moved up to work with Ho on the China-Vietnam border at Bac Po, which proved to be a tragic decision for his young wife and daughter. While Giap was gone, the French imprisoned his wife and daughter; while in prison they both perished. This tragedy would leave an emotional scar on Giap and increase his resolve to defeat the French.

Nguyen Thi Minh Khai (1901–1941).

Vietminh military tactics against the French were primarily unconventional. Spies infiltrated the Hanoi homes of French military leaders. Giap insisted that the rural population be politically educated so they could understand the difference between DRV rule and a French colonial government. French soldiers feared leaving the urban centers because of the Vietminh's effective guerilla warfare. Vietminh soldiers used the highlands as bases from which they could launch surprise attacks against the French. The Vietnamese were patient soldiers and time was on their side.

Propaganda poster placed in northern villages during the First Indochina War. It was meant to encourage mass education.

Contemporary water colors that depict the peasants' attempts to defeat the French during the First Indochina War

France and Vietnam were not the only countries at war between 1946 and 1954. In truth, this war was a sidelight to much larger conflicts. In China, the civil war between the Nationalists and Communists resulted in the ousting of the Nationalists and in Mao Zedong's founding of the Communist People's Republic of China in late 1949. One year later, North Korea, a client of the Soviet Union, attacked South Korea, a client of the United States. In Europe the Iron Curtain divided Europe along ideological and economic lines. The Cold War had begun. Suddenly, the battles in Vietnam had global implications. The United States, in particular, was keenly interested in halting the spread of Communism in Asia. The Eisenhower-Nixon administrations dramatically increased American aid to the French forces in northern Vietnam.

Dien Bien Phu (1954)

French military leaders were anxious to fight a conventional battle with the Vietminh. They believed that if they could lure the DRV into an open conflict, then France's superior weaponry and tactics would prevail. The Vietminh accepted the challenge and decided to bait the French to fight in the town of Dien Bien Phu. General Giap began to send troops into the northwestern portion of Laos, knowing that the French would respond to this intrusion. The French commander, General Henri Navarre, ordered 15,000 French troops to occupy the town of Dien Bien Phu, which was located in a valley close to the Laos-Vietnam border. The showdown was set. Navarre believed that he held the advantage in this battle because the town was surrounded by high mountains, which meant that it would be difficult, if not impossible, for the Vietminh to haul heavy long-range cannons

Ho Chi Minh and other party leaders looking over battle plans for Dien Bien Phu. At the extreme right stands General Vo Nguyen Giap.

The Vietminh overrunning the French fortifications at Dien Bien Phu.

over the steep mountain passes. The French also believed they would be able to use airplanes to bomb the Vietminh. These assumptions were false and would cost the French dearly.

By sheer will and muscle, the Vietminh were able to bring heavy cannons over the steep mountains. Once in place and pointed directly at the French garrisons, these weapons were undetectable because of the thick mountain foliage. The advantage that airpower might have given the French proved illusory because of the dense fog that often covered the valley. Combined with the intense storms of the monsoon season, it was virtually impossible for airplanes to drop supplies to the beleaguered French forces in the town. Moreover, the Vietminh were undetectable behind the flora that characterized the mountain landscape, and so the air bombing campaigns that were supposed to make the difference in this conventional battle never occurred. On May 6, 1954, the French Army at Dien Bien Phu surrendered to the Vietminh. One day later, scheduled talks between the DRV and the French began in Geneva, Switzerland.

The Geneva Accords

The DRV victory at Dien Bien Phu was the greatest defeat of a Western colonial army in Asia. Armed with this victory, the DRV representatives arrived in Geneva believing that their military triumphs would result in political successes at the negotiation table. They were wrong. Weeks passed at Geneva with all sides at an impasse. France's citizens were frustrated with what they termed the "dirty war" in Vietnam. The French parliament ousted the intransigent Prime Minister Laniel, and voted in Mendès-France, who guaranteed to arrive at an agreement at Geneva within the first four weeks of his new administration.

This intensified the pressure on the French negotiators. Within this context, the amiable Chinese representative, Zhou En-lai, began to work behind the scenes with the French to broker an agreement. Once the two achieved a consensus, they presented the deal to the Vietminh delegation. Shocked and disappointed by the terms of the accord, the DRV officials believed that China had betrayed them. With no other ally, the DRV signed the agreement.

The terms were as follows: both France and DRV troops would halt their hostilities; Vietnam would be divided at the sixteenth parallel (it was renegotiated to make it the seventeenth parallel); the DRV would politically control the northern portion of Vietnam, while the South would remain under the control of Emperor Bao Dai's anti-communist government—the Republic of Vietnam (RVN); and the unification of Vietnam would be determined through a national plebiscite conducted no longer than two years after the Geneva meeting. Even more injurious for the DRV, Zhou Enlai hinted that China wished to open up relations with South Vietnam. This set the stage for the Second Indochina War.

The Second Indochina War (1965–1973)

France was through with Vietnam. They could not get out of the region fast enough. This withdrawal left the RVN in an extremely vulnerable position. Ho Chi Minh's popularity had reached into southern Vietnam and the Vietminh were an experienced military force that could easily overwhelm its southern rivals. Emperor Bao Dai remained in France, and the RVN appeared to be a fledgling short-lived phenomena. It probably

Mao Zedong's establishment of the People's Republic of China made the U.S. more interested in Vietnam. To the extreme right is the PRC's premier, Zhou Enlai.

would have succumbed to northern pressure had not the United States stepped into the picture.

President Ngo Dinh Diem (1901–1963)

A priority for the United States was to find a DRV leader with whom it could work. American officials believed they found that special man and pressured Emperor Bao Dai to appoint Ngo Dinh Diem as RVN prime minister. Diem was somewhat of a strange choice: he grew up around the imperial palace at Hue; he was a devout Catholic in a Buddhist land; and he was a lawyer who eschewed politics after the Vietminh assassinated his brother. After World War II, he moved to the United States where he sought religious solitude. The U.S. was fond of Diem because of his staunch anti-communist stand. Various American Catholic leaders were also attracted to Diem because of his religious affiliations.

After just a year in office, Diem orchestrated an election that removed Bao Dai as the RVN's supreme leader. This was a turning point for Diem. Behind an election mandate where he reportedly received 98.2 percent of the votes, and with massive economic aid from the United States, Diem was in a position to make positive changes for southern Vietnam. Yet, Diem was steeped in Confucian values and his primary concern was for family members and the landed elite. Thus, while the Vietminh preached economic equity, Diem allowed the rich business people and large landowners to increase their wealth at the expense of the peasants. He appointed his brother, Ngo Dinh Nhu, as Minister of the Interior. Nhu and his wife, Madame Nhu, actively persecuted every southern Vietnam organization that criticized the DRV Government. They quickly became the most unpopular figures in the DRV Government. Despite pleas from American advisors to replace Nhu, Diem insisted that his brother and sister-in-law were doing a superb job.

In North Vietnam, the Vietminh leadership correctly anticipated that the U.S. and Diem would ignore the Geneva demand that a plebiscite take place in 1956. Ho Chi Minh's priority after Geneva was to consolidate the northern region and improve the wore-torn economy. The DRV instituted a policy that redistributed land away from the rich to the poor. When this strategy met resistance, numerous large landowners were killed. The problem of land shortage in the DRV was alleviated when more than one million northern Catholics followed their priests onto U.S. transport ships into South Vietnam. The DRV redistributed the land and villages abandoned by the Catholics to its landless citizens. North Vietnam also received limited aid from the Soviet Union and China as the Cold War heated up.

To pressure Diem's government, North Vietnam created the National Liberation Front (NLF) in the South. This secret organization was ordered to spread communist ideology throughout the RVN's rural villages. Because of Diem's policies, the NLF found a sympathetic audience for its message. It is estimated that by 1963, two-thirds of the RVN's villages were controlled by the NLF. Diem and his allies controlled the urban areas of the RVN. However, due to the limited freedom in the South, prisons filled up with students and anti-government protestors. As objections to his rule increased, Diem blamed all the problems on communist sympathizers. The pejorative term placed on all the anti-government elements was "Vietcong." In fact, not all the anti-government personnel were sympathetic to the NLF. However, as Diem and Nhu increased their power and harsh policies, many of these individuals did join the communist insurgents.

Increased U.S. Involvement

To offset the NLF gains, the United States established the Military Assistance Command in Vietnam (MACV). Hoping to reverse the trends in the rural areas, MACV personnel worked with the RVN government to create Communist-free villages. This plan was labeled the Hamlet Program. While the strategy was well-intentioned, it was not thought through properly. First, thousands of farmers had to provide free labor for the construction of these hamlets. Yet, when a settlement was completed, it could not accommodate all the people who had constructed it. Thus, farmers provided labor for something from which they would not benefit. These newly constructed villages were surrounded by barbed wire and villagers were told they were now truly free because the NLF would not be able to penetrate the villages at night. This situation effectively restricted rather than expanded the peasants' freedom. Finally, in a culture where ancestors are revered, many southern peasants were forced to move off of lands where they had meticulously cared for their parents and grandparents' graves. United States advisors tried to alleviate these difficulties by introducing new farming equipment, medical support, and strains of rice that would increase farm production.

These misguided countryside policies did not improve Diem's popularity. He was convinced that he had Vietnam's best interest in mind, and he believed his critics simply did not comprehend the complexities involved in administrating the RVN. In the Confucian ideal, Diem was a virtuous leader. He never married and devoted his time to overseeing his bureaucracy. He remained devoted to his family and his faith. His entire family was Catholic, and one of his brothers was the Bishop of Hue.

Catholicism was not the dominant religion of Vietnam, however, and as the insurgency movement in the South grew in scope, any organization not in line with Diem became a target for persecution. This included the popular Cao Dai and Hoa Hao faiths. But it was the Buddhist religion that bore the brunt of persecution at the hands of Diem's family. Throughout 1963 ARVN raids were conducted against Buddhist temples, and reporters caught the brutality on film. A dramatic event took place on June 11, 1963, when a Buddhist priest immolated himself in the center of Saigon to protest the RVN's persecution of the Buddhist faith. Rather than show sympathy toward the Buddhists, Diem's sister-in-law Madame Nhu noted at a news conference that these sacrifices were nothing more than "barbecues." U.S. advisors encouraged Diem to be more sympathetic toward the Buddhists, and hinted that he should replace Nhu with someone more in touch with the Vietnamese people.

As Diem's popularity continued to wane, military leaders in the Army of the Republic of Vietnam began to plot an overthrow of the government. Some of these leaders approached U.S. advisors to gauge what the U.S. response would be to a military coup. To many of the ARVN officers' surprise, American officials indicated that they would look forward to working with a new administration.

President Diem knew that there were people in his government who were planning a coup. He also was aware that these plots would not come to fruition without the consent of the United States. In an August 7, 1963 interview with

Marguerite Higgins, an American journalist in Saigon, Diem expressed these sentiments:

> But now I hear hints that this aid may be withdrawn if I do not do exactly what the Americans demand. Isn't there a certain arrogance in these demands? America has a magnificent economy and many good points. But does your strength at home automatically mean that the United States is entitled to dictate everything here in Vietnam, which is undergoing a type of war that your country has never experienced? If you order Vietnam around like a puppet on a string, how will you be different—except in degree—from the French? I am not unaware that some Americans are flirting with elements in my country that perennially plot against me. These elements cannot succeed without the Americans, and they know it.

A few months later, on November 1, 1963, generals from the ARVN took control of the government. The following day Diem and Nhu were murdered while in ARVN custody. President Kennedy expressed outrage at this turn of events, unaware that in a short time he himself would join Diem in death.

In a matter of weeks there was a shift in leadership both in the Republic of Vietnam and in the United States. American advisors hoped that these changes would reverse the NLF gains in South Vietnam. In fact, what they found was that the ARVN leaders were easier to control than Diem, but there were problems that pervaded RVN's society and military. United States aid to the RVN was matched by increases in supplies and men from North Vietnam. The North Vietnamese constructed a hidden path from the North to the South which wound its way through portions of neighboring Laos and Cambodia. The so-called Ho Chi Minh Trail was a source of frustration for U.S. and RVN military commanders. The trail was impossible to see from the air because of the dense foliage. This prevented any type of effective bombing, though the U.S. did bomb the areas they thought were part of the trail. However, in the end, Ho's enemies could not prevent North Vietnamese troops from slipping into the South.

President Johnson and the Tonkin Gulf Incident (1964)

In 1964 U.S. President Lyndon Johnson had a difficult choice to make. He had inherited a decade's worth of paradoxical policies. For ten years, since the Geneva Accords, the United States had done just about everything it could to support the fledgling RVN Government. Large amounts of money and supplies were making their way to South Vietnam daily. American military, political, and social advisors were sent to the RVN to increase the effectiveness of the RVN government. More importantly for American politicians, Vietnam became the symbol that America would not allow democratic countries to fall into the hands of the evil communist empire. For American business people, South Vietnam represented a place to take a stand for the free market system. American officials claimed that if South Vietnam succumbed to Communism, then all the other nations would fall like dominos to this anti-God, anti-free market ideology. What was paradoxical about these policies was that the more America tried to help the RVN, the worse the situation became.

It seemed clear that there were two options Johnson had in 1964 with regard to South Vietnam. First, he could cut losses and withdraw personnel and economic aid to the Southeast Asian state. In hindsight, many believe this is what the United States should have done. However, it must be remembered that by 1964 America had not only invested economic aid to the RVN, but it also had staked its global reputation as a country that does not abandon democracies. The second road America could choose was to increase its presence in South Vietnam, an option that included sending American combat troops to fight the Vietminh and the Vietcong. President Johnson listened to his advisors, and the council was mixed. Both sides had valid arguments. Yet, it appears that the dice were cast in the waters of the Tonkin Gulf.

During August 1964, American ships increased their presence in North Vietnamese waters as they provided support for clandestine ARVN maneuvers on islands off the DRV coast. North Vietnamese patrol boats tried to drive off the much larger U.S. ships in the Tonkin Gulf. After destroying these Vietminh boats, the U.S. ships withdrew but were then ordered to return with several more ships for support. While it has never been confirmed, American radar operators on the ships claimed that they were under attack from the North Vietnamese as they returned. This claim prompted President Johnson to order the bombing of North Vietnam. The United States Congress passed the Gulf of Tonkin Resolution, which gave the President authority to do all in his power to stop any aggression against United States personnel in Vietnam. In essence, it was a blank check for the President. He approved increased bombing raids on North Vietnam and eventually ordered U.S. troops to fight in Vietnam.

While the RVN was grateful for this new support, Ho Chi Minh and the DRV were taken aback at these developments. The Twelfth Plenum of the Central Committee met in Hanoi during December 1965. The DRV generals and officials determined that it would match the United States' determination. They resolved that the war would not be considered over until Vietnam was united.

North Vietnam had two things going for it. First, history demonstrated that foreign powers eventually lose their grip on Vietnam. This had happened to China, Japan, and France. While the United States was the greatest military power on the planet, Washington D.C. was 10,000 miles away from Hanoi. During its war with France, the Vietminh had established effective guerilla warfare and had even defeated France in the one major conventional battle of the war: Dien Bien Phu. Second, DRV leadership was also encouraged by the support they received from the Soviet Union and the People's Republic of China (PRC). While these two great nations were at odds with each other in the 1960s, they both agreed to support North Vietnam's war effort. Thus North and South Vietnam became pawns in a much larger game.

At the outset of hostilities, there was a window of opportunity for negotiations between Hanoi and Washington. However, both parties insisted that certain terms be met before serious talks could begin. Ho Chi Minh asserted that America halt its bombing campaigns before he would listen to American ideas for peace in Vietnam. For its part, the U.S. claimed that it would not hold serious talks with the DRV until it stopped sending men and material into South Vietnam via the Ho Chi Minh trail. Neither condition was met, and bloody conflict resulted. By 1967 there were more than half a million U.S. troops in South Vietnam.

The Devastation of War

More than a million Vietnamese lost their lives during the U.S.-Vietnam War, while the United States lost over 60,000 personnel in this conflict. The human tragedy extended beyond the loss of life. Vietnam's environment suffered because of the war. American planes sprinkled the land with napalm to reduce the foliage in which Vietminh and Vietcong soldiers hid. Chemicals dropped from U.S. planes poisoned Vietnam's soil. Both South and North Vietnam's economies and societies were transformed by this war.

South Vietnam's rural farmers and their families were devastated. They were in a no-win situation. Because they represented the majority of the South's population, there was a contest between the U.S. and the DRV to capture their loyalty. Neutrality was impossible: if they did not show support to one side, they were labeled as traitors. Vietminh, ARVN, U.S., and NLF personnel murdered village leaders, as well as rank-and-file farmers. Simple farming became a dangerous occupation in South Vietnam.

More than four million rural folk moved into the RVN urban centers, transforming these cities. The economy in South Vietnam's cities revolved around the money U.S. troops spent for rest and relaxation. In Saigon, the service-sector of the economy flourished. Many of the young American soldiers flocked to Saigon during their period of rest and relaxation with the hopes of forgetting the war—even if for just one evening. Prostitution, a black market of foreign goods, and overcrowded streets characterized Saigon during the conflict. Young women sold their bodies to keep their families financially afloat. In short, South Vietnam's society was turned on its head.

North Vietnam's economy and society were also transformed because of the war. During the 1950s, the DRV leadership had followed the Chinese pattern of taking land away from the rich and giving it to the poor. Since it was the pattern of the

Prison cell that is part of a current exhibition at Hoa Lo Prison. Originally built by the French in 1896, the prison housed captured American pilots from August 5, 1964 to March 31, 1973.

American P.O.W.

PRC, it was followed by the DRV, even though this meant the elimination of an entire class of landowners. In China, however, the redistribution of land did not produce the dramatic economic results for which Mao had hoped. During 1959 Mao launched the radical economic program entitled the Great Leap Forward, where private property was abolished and the entire population was called to work in large communes where life was regulated "for the good of the nation." The DRV believed that similar radical action was needed based on the crisis in the South. Between 1958 and 1964, the majority of North Vietnamese farmers lost their private plots of land and were incorporated into more than 30,000 different agricultural cooperatives. In each cooperative roughly eighty-five families worked in concert to produce food for the government.

By the early 1960s, the DRV had become aware of the growing animosity between the Soviet Union and the PRC, and it tried to play each off the other. For its part, the DRV began to lean toward the less radical Soviet advisors because of the success of the power plants and other industrial complexes that the USSR helped to build in the DRV. Communism was not going to prosper by rhetoric, the Russians persuaded the Vietnamese, and Mao's radical view of continual revolution was not producing economic prosperity in the PRC.

As early as 1965, various American journalists predicted that the Vietnam War would become a nightmare for the United States. In that year David Halberstam published his insightful study, *The Making of a Quagmire*. His forecast was correct. In Vietnam, the ARVN troops were discouraged due to corruption among their generals. Many of its units were undermanned because ARVN leaders had larger detachments on paper than they did in the field. They kept up this ruse so they could receive supplies and payment for soldiers that did not exist. Drug-use and racial tensions were some of the difficulties facing U.S. troops in Vietnam. There was a sense among these soldiers that the enemy was unidentifiable—it might be an old farmer or a teenage boy. Furthermore, the objectives for the U.S. troops were unclear. They would take one area, at a great cost of life, only to see it slip back into enemy hands.

Opposition to the war also increased in the United States, particularly at universities. America was experiencing a cultural revolution and beginning to question the reasons that soldiers and civilians were dying. The U.S. press correctly reported that the RVN Government was in chaos and needed an overhaul. In response to this, the South Vietnamese created a new constitution in 1967 that provided for open elections. However, freedom of expression remained limited and anti-war Buddhist candidates were denied the right to run for office. Nguyen Van Thieu, a former ARVN general, won the election and would remain the political leader of the RVN until days before the fall of South Vietnam in 1975.

The Tet Offensive (1968)

Many believe the turning point of the Vietnam War took place in the early hours of January 31, 1968. This date was the beginning of the Lunar New Year's celebration in Vietnam, also known as Tet. In a coordinated maneuver, NLF and Vietminh forces attacked the urban areas of South Vietnam. They believed that the general population would join this uprising and force America to withdraw from Vietnam. This major offensive was, at the same time, the greatest victory and the worst defeat for the communist forces.

In terms of military planning, the Tet Offensive was a disaster for the Vietcong forces, which made up the majority of the communist personnel during these attacks. Heavy casualties among Vietcong forces forced them to surrender any early gains they had made in the cities. One exception to this was the city of Hue, where Vietminh forces were able to hold the city for two weeks. That was the extent of the military accomplishments of this offensive. The general uprising that the NLF was expecting did not materialize. This apathy was a greater disappointment for the Tet planners than their military failures. It seems improbable given these facts that the Tet Offensive also proved to be one of the NLF's greatest successes. The reason for this has to do with the media.

The Vietnam War was one of the first "television wars." People around the world could follow the conflict on the news as journalists and camera crews provided daily stories and images. During the Tet Offensive, television crews filmed American personnel scurrying out of the U.S. embassy, which the Vietcong forces occupied for several hours. Other images captured on film during Tet included an ARVN officer summarily executing a member of the Vietcong.

These pictures sent shock waves through the United States. Many Americans assumed that their army was on the verge of winning the Vietnam War. Walter Cronkite, the most popular American broadcaster in 1968, concluded that Tet demonstrated America could only hope for a stalemate in Vietnam. Tet also had an effect on President Johnson's advisors, who questioned the wisdom of sending more troops to a war in a country that held no promise of victory. President Johnson decided that he would not seek or accept his party's nomination for the 1968 presidential election, leaving the morass of Vietnam for the next president.

In North Vietnam, the party was given an unrealistic picture of the Tet Offensive. Losses were minimized in the report, and many Vietcong believed that they had been used as fodder in this campaign. This perception increased the distrust between southern Communists and the DRV. These problems were not brought up when the final report of the Tet Offensive was written. What the document clearly stated, however, was that fighting in the South would continue indefinitely:

> Although the enemy is suffering defeat and is in a passive and confused situation, he still has strength and is very stubborn. In his death throes he will resort to more murderous and savage actions. . . . The struggle between the enemy and us will become fiercer, particularly in areas adjoining the towns and cities. . . . However, it must be clearly realized that this will be but the enemy's convulsions before death, his reaction from a weak, not a strong position. The situation will continue to develop in a way favorable to us and detrimental to the enemy with the possibility of sudden developments which we must be ready to take advantage of in order to secure final victory.

One reason DRV leaders might have given for launching the Tet Offensive was that Ho Chi Minh's health was precarious, and there was a desire to unite Vietnam before his death. By the late 1960s, Ho spent much of his time receiving medical attention in China. Le Duan (1908–1986) was elected General Secretary of the party in 1960 and was the central figure in North Vietnam's political scene. When Ho Chi Minh died on September 2, 1969, Le Duan's influence in the DRV Government increased.

President Nixon and the Peace Talks

In late 1968 the United States elected Richard Nixon to be its thirty-sixth president. He campaigned on the promise that he would bring an honorable peace to Vietnam. During the 1950s, Richard Nixon had visited Vietnam as Vice-President. In his earlier political career, he attacked his opponents as individuals who were too soft on Communism. Now as president, Nixon brought in an advisor, Henry Kissinger, and together they planned to bring peace to Vietnam.

Peace negotiations began in 1969 in Paris, France. The meetings included representatives from North and South Vietnam, the U.S., and the NLFV. Nixon and Kissinger were frustrated by the intransigence of the North Vietnamese negotiators. They believed that if they could increase their victories in Vietnam it would convince the North Vietnamese that they must compromise their demands. Within this context, the war entered a new phase in 1970.

The U.S. President and his advisor believed that the reason for the NLF success was that the Communists had a large base in neighboring Cambodia. This illusive center was known as the Central Office for South Vietnam (COSVN). Nixon and Kissinger assumed that if they could destroy this Cambodian-based communist station, then U.S. troops would have greater success in South Vietnam. However, they found it difficult to get the Cambodian leader, Norodom Sihanouk, to accept U.S. military plans during the Vietnam War.

Extremely popular among his people, Sihanouk had steered his country through numerous storms in the 1950s and 1960s. He openly admitted that his policy toward the Vietnam War was

Le Duan at Ho Chi Minh's memorial ceremony.

one of neutrality. This stance frustrated the Americans and ARVN because they believed that Vietminh agents were hiding in Cambodian territory. Frustration finally led to action. On March 18, 1970, President Nixon and Henry Kissinger decided to begin secret bombing operations in Cambodian territory. While the immediate results of this secret bombing campaign were minimal, the consequences of this decision would prove disastrous in later years.

Sihanouk protested these bombing raids, but while he was on a trip outside of Cambodia a coup pushed him out of power. The Cambodian government was now directed by pro-American elements in the Cambodian military. ARVN and American troops invaded Cambodia but found that the so-called huge North Vietnamese bases did not exist—or could not be found. An important outcome of these actions was that the miniscule communist element in Cambodia, the Khmer Rouge, received legitimacy from the exiled Sihanouk, who called on the Cambodian people to reject the pro-American puppet government and to align with the Khmer Rouge.

After years of negotiating, the United States and North Vietnam came to an agreement on January 27, 1973. The U.S. agreed to withdraw its military personnel from South Vietnam. North Vietnam could keep its troops in South Vietnam as long as it recognized the Thieu government. Also, an exchange of prisoners would complete the agreement.

President Thieu was not consulted on major points of the accord. The RVN believed that it had been betrayed by a country that had promised it would never leave or forsake South Vietnam. In fact, on April 30, 1975, less than two years following the Paris agreement, North Vietnamese troops marched into

Saigon and deposed the RVN government. Just thirteen days before, the Khmer Rouge army had marched into Cambodia's capital of Phnom Penh and ousted Lon Nol's pro-American government.

The Socialist Republic
of Vietnam (1976)

Growing Pains

In 1975 there were many reasons for the Vietnamese to be proud. For the first time in more than 100 years the country was unified. During that period it had successfully rebuffed French, Chinese, Japanese, and American armies. Yet the Vietnamese knew that there were going to be growing pains in the process of reunification. Southerners feared that they would be punished for their collaboration with the United States. Uncertainty hung in the air.

While the DRV leaders celebrated Vietnam's unification, they were also faced with a war-tattered economy. In the North, twenty-nine out of thirty provincial capitals were damaged, and nine of those were completely destroyed. In the South, the economy and society were centered in the American-supported service sectors of the urban areas. One observer described the situation in these terms:

> The legacy of the U.S.-Thieu regime was an economic and social malaise of unknown proportion: an economy that was on the verge of bankruptcy; a threatening famine in the northern provinces of Central Vietnam; more than three million unemployed people, excluding the army of a half-million prostitutes about to be out of work; six to

seven million refugees who had been forced by wartime activities to flee their native villages into the cities, etc.

DRV leaders sought to produce a feeling of unity and renamed the country the Socialist Republic of Vietnam (SRV) in 1976. Hanoi was adopted as the SRV capital, and Saigon was renamed Ho Chi Minh City. Southerners learned that there would not be a wholesale extermination of those who had collaborated with the United States. However, Communist officials did set up reeducation camps for former ARVN soldiers, RVN officials, and prostitutes. Internees were required to farm in the daytime, while attending lessons on Marxism in the evenings. Many languished in these camps for years, and international groups protested against the demeaning aspects of these outdoor prisons. Seven years after these camps were established, there were still more than 120,000 Vietnamese locked up in them.

These hard-labor facilities were just one part of a revamping program for South Vietnam. To force people out of the overcrowded cities, special economic zones were created. During 1976 more than 600,000 people were required to leave Ho Chi Minh City and settle on these new farms. Many of these places were carved out of mosquito-infested swamps.

Two other South Vietnam groups experienced hardship after 1975. Paradoxically, the NLF, Vietcong, and the provisional government that the southern Communists had established were pushed aside by the more dominant Northern officials. Southern cadres who had sacrificed for years believed that the North ignored all their efforts. Thus, longstanding animosity between northern and southern peoples did not die with the formation of the SRV.

Finally, Chinese business people were stripped of their property. There were several reasons for this action. First, the

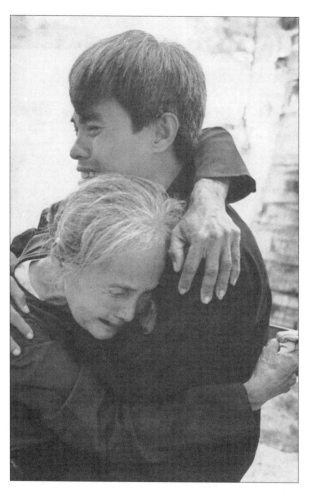

A Vietnamese mother from the North finding her son from the South after Vietnam's reunification on April 30, 1975.

Chinese owned many of the successful private businesses in South Vietnam. The SRV intended to move the country to a state-controlled economy and they believed private enterprise was akin to capitalism. It was also during this period that relations between Vietnam and China reached a new low. During 1976 the SRV Government made a decision to side with the Soviet Union in the continuing China-Soviet Cold War. Two years later, Chinese citizens in Vietnam were told that they could no longer enjoy dual citizenship.

These policies created a group of people anxious to leave Vietnam. However, as it was illegal to leave Vietnam without permission from the State, thousands of people began to buy their way on to boats that would take them to Hong Kong, Thailand, Malaysia, the Philippines—anywhere outside of the Vietnam area. Heartbreaking stories of the "boat people" began to emerge from this situation. At times the boats would be adrift for days with little or no food and water for its passengers. It was not unusual for a boat to be stopped by pirates. These bandits robbed the passengers and raped the women. Furthermore, tales of persecution and hardship in Vietnam made the SRV Government an international pariah. The United States made sure that world financial institutions and nations trading with the U.S. would not provide any aid to Vietnam. These sanctions caused Vietnam to rely even more heavily on the Soviet Union's support, and Vietnam limped along with a wrecked economy.

The Vietnamese-Cambodian War (1975–1989)

One of the SRV's first major external crises was with its western neighbor, Cambodia. After the Khmer Rouge gained control of

A Russian engineer explains the plans for a power plant in South Vietnam—a consequence of Vietnam's choice to draw closer to the Soviet Union after 1975.

Cambodia, it instituted a radical policy of an agrarian utopia. Cities were emptied and all Cambodians were forced to work in rural communes. Brutality marked the Khmer Rouge government, and some estimate that one-third of that country's populace died between 1975 and 1978. Pol Pot and other Khmer Rouge leaders received economic aid from China. Meanwhile, Khmer Rouge soldiers increased their incursions into Vietnamese territory. Several Cambodian soldiers fled to Vietnam telling stories about Khmer Rouge extermination policies and mass starvation. On December 25, 1978, Vietnam finally invaded its neighbor and, in three weeks, it pushed the Khmer Rouge out of Cambodia and into refugee camps on the Thai-Cambodia border.

The United Nations, China, and every country that the United States could pressure condemned Vietnam for this invasion. In February 1979, China demonstrated its displeasure by invading Vietnam. The fight between these countries was brief but costly for both sides. Vietnam did not withdraw from Cambodia, remaining only through the economic support it received from the Soviet Union. In fact, Vietnam faced the same dilemmas that the United States military had faced during the 1960s. If Vietnam withdrew from Cambodia, the Khmer Rouge would return and take control of the government. Sensitive to the accusation of being an imperialist country, Vietnam set up a government in Phnom Penh that was composed of pro-Vietnamese Cambodians. For a decade the Vietnamese army occupied Cambodia.

With a weak economy, the only way Vietnam was able to sustain its operations in Cambodia was by massive support from the Soviet Union. Vietnam was the USSR's proxy in its continued hostilities against the PRC, while the Khmer Rouge

Vietnamese pilots return from exercises during Vietnam's war with Cambodia.

remained China's surrogate in its battle against Vietnam and the Soviet Union. But it is dangerous to rely so heavily on one source for aid. The SRV realized this in 1989, as Mikhail Gorbachev began dismantling the Soviet Union. In June 1989 Gorbachev visited China. The PRC leadership insisted that normal relations between China and Russia were predicated on Vietnam's withdrawal from Cambodia. Vietnam was forced to withdraw from Cambodia, but, with the help of the United Nations, a government was set up in Phnom Penh that proved to be friendly to Vietnam.

The *Doi Moi* Experiment (1986)

Ten years after its reunification, it was apparent that Vietnam's state-run economy was not producing an improved living standard for its people. This was particularly true for the farmers, which still made up close to seventy percent of the population. Agriculture production, which was projected to increase at an annual rate of eighteen percent, actually decreased during the early 1980s. There were reports of malnutrition and famine in the northern portions of the country. What made this even more tragic was the fact that the SRV intended to use its projected agricultural exports to finance the industrialization of the country.

Officials were shocked at the state of Vietnam's economy. Their optimistic post-1975 predictions were rooted in the resolve of the Vietnamese people. They reasoned that if their countrymen could defeat the planet's greatest powers, then surely they could develop a strong economy. Unfortunately, these same leaders implemented changes that resulted in Vietnam's dire economic straights.

When the Communist leaders united Vietnam, they were committed to erasing exploitation and financial greed. As such, they determined that all farmland should be transformed into agricultural cooperatives. Farmers were commanded to pool their labor, tools, and land in these cooperatives. Private ownership of land was considered diametrically opposed to the government's sentiment of socialism. Likewise, privately-owned businesses were either closed or turned into state-owned enterprises. These policies were intended to help Vietnam's economy, but they did the opposite. Farmers complained that there was no incentive to be creative or work hard because all farmers received a similar stipend from the government. Similarly, incompetent communist cadres, who were ideologically pure but lacked the basic knowledge to successfully administer a factory, replaced the nation's brightest entrepreneurs.

By 1982, the SRV was forced to reevaluate its plans. They permitted farmers to subcontract portions of Vietnam's agriculture cooperative farmland. Families paid the state a certain amount to work this soil. However, the subcontracting agreement allowed the farmers to keep or sell any surplus grain. There is a hint of capitalism in the subcontract system.

Nonetheless, Vietnamese families generated an income outside of the state-sanctioned cooperative. Families also began to make handicrafts at home that were sold in open markets. Entrepreneurial farmers received permission to raise animals and sell them at market prices. By 1983, the private funds from these activities supplied up to sixty percent of Vietnamese farmers' revenues. The country's population was slowly weaning itself from state handouts.

By the end of 1985, there was reason to believe that the subcontracting system had pulled Vietnam out of its economic nosedive. Agricultural production had monetarily increased by more than 30 percent, while the availability of food had increased by twenty percent. Rice paddies' production rose by more than thirty percent. Despite these amazing numbers, the SRV faced even more difficult economic trials in 1985 than it had five years earlier.

Vietnam's population grew at an astounding 13.8 percent between 1980 and 1985. This development offset Vietnam's economic gains. In fact, the optimistic financial predictions of Vietnam's top officials proved false. In 1976, the Vietnamese were assured that in ten years every home would have a radio set, a refrigerator, and a television set. At the end of that period, families were fortunate to have one of these products in their home.

By UN estimations, Vietnam's per capita income was $101 in 1976. It had slipped to $91 in 1980 and rebounded slightly to $99 by 1982. In 1985, health officials estimated that the Vietnamese peasants were receiving less than eighty percent of their daily needed calories. During the same year, infant birth weights dropped to alarmingly low levels. Foreign medical workers estimated that during the year 1985, ten percent of Vietnam's children died from gastro-enteritis. Malnutrition is a primary cause of this malady.

In December 1986, Vietnam's Communist Party (VCP) held its sixth congress. The meeting was a surprisingly frank discussion about the SRV economic failures. Top VCP officials retired because of the disastrous state-controlled economy. Several officials commented that the only economic bright spot in Vietnam was the subcontracting system. The socialist transformation of the economy was declared a failure, and the party established a new renovation program termed *doi moi*. This initiative attacked the centrally-planned economy. Its goal was to take the entrepreneurial spirit of the farmers and extend it to other areas of Vietnam's society and economy.

An immediate consequence of *doi moi* was that the government allowed individuals to create businesses for profit. The SRV also lowered foreign and domestic trade restrictions. State-owned factories, most of which were not profitable, were notified that government subsidies would eventually be eliminated. Businesses would succeed or fail based on entrepreneurial activities—a very capitalistic sounding notion.

These ambitious reforms ran into immediate problems. First, state-run factory managers were not trained to function in an open market system. Apart from the factory administrators, millions of workers dependent on state employment had to find jobs. In the mid-1980s, unemployment and underemployment reached their highest levels in Vietnam's recent history. At the same time period, inflation plagued the country's economy. The banking system was also beleaguered by the government's monetary and economic policies. Inflation and a decline in food production caused near-famine conditions for three million Vietnamese during this period.

Today, SRV officials continue to accelerate the *doi moi* policies. However, the country's communist leaders are unable to reconcile a free market economy with other freedoms such as religion, speech, and a free press. Nonetheless, Vietnam continues to seek greater participation in a global economy. Unfortunately, bureaucratic fraud means that very few foreign companies have had a positive experience in Vietnam. Incessant corruption by local, regional, and national officials hinder Vietnam's supposed free-market system.

One example of the frustration local and foreign investors experience is evidenced in the highly anticipated Vietnam Stock

A Ho Chi Minh barber, one of the many Vietnamese entrepreneurs who set up shop on the sidewalk.

Vietnamese women making conical palm hats, an important economic sideline project throughout the country.

Market. After promising that such an organization would be a reality, government officials opened the nation's first stock market in late July 2000. There were only two firms that were listed at the Securities Trading Center: Refrigeration Electrical Engineering, and Cables and Telecommunications Material. On the first day of trading, only four thousand shares were exchanged because the government placed a ceiling on the price of the shares. The continued government intervention in Vietnam's stock market has left most investors skeptical of the economic viability of the organization.

Thus, while Vietnam is economically in a much better position than it was during the 1980s, it continues to limp behind even its weakest neighbors. If it is to have a vibrant economy, the SRV will have to commit to a truly free market system. For this to happen, the VCP will have to further separate itself from the state's economic system. Until this happens, Vietnam's economic direction will remain in limbo.

A Tale of Two Artists

Vietnam's art, like its language and food, is unique. Many of its greatest art pieces, whether in the field of literature, paintings, songs, or architectural structures, are relatively new works. Because of perpetual wars, Vietnam does not have ancient magnificent architectural structures like the neighboring Angkor Wat temples of Cambodia. There are also very few Vietnamese paintings that date back more than two hundred years. Throughout most of Vietnam's past, artists exclusively created their work for religious institutes. The emphasis on religious art began to change in the twentieth century, mainly because of foreign influence.

One aspect of French rule in Vietnam was the establishment of art institutes in Hanoi and Saigon. The most prestigious art school was the Ecole des Beaux-Arts de l'Indochine. This school was founded by the French painter Victor Tardieu. During its twenty years of existence, the school graduated 128 painters and sculptors. Today, Vietnamese painters are exhibited in galleries around the world. Some of the more noted painters' works are shown in Singapore and Hong Kong galleries.

Van Cao (1923–1994)

Van Cao, author of Vietnam's national anthem.

Van Cao was Vietnam's premiere twentieth-century poet and lyricists. Born on November 15, 1923, Van Cao grew up in the northern port city of Haiphong, and his songs are filled with allusions to the sea. He began writing songs, most of them were romantic, as a teenager. These include "Sadness at the End of Autumn," "Eden," "The Shore of Spring," and "Dreamy Stream."

During World War II, Van Cao studied at the Indochinese Art School in Hanoi. His abilities extended to drawing and playing various instruments. The devastation of war caused him to join the Vietminh. He moved to Viet Bac, near the Chinese border, and he was asked by his comrades to write a song to bolster their spirits. He penned, "Forward March."

Soldiers of Vietnam, we go forward,
With the one will to save our Fatherland.
Our hurried steps are sounding on the long and arduous
    road.
Our flag, red with the blood of victory, bears the spirit of
    our country.
The distant rumbling of the guns mingles with our
    marching song.
The path to glory passes over the bodies of our foes.
Overcoming all hardships, together we build our
    resistance bases.
Ceaselessly for the people's cause we struggle,
Hastening to the battle field!
Forward! All together advancing!
Our Vietnam is strong eternal.

Soldiers of Vietnam, we go forward,
The gold star of our flag in the wind.
Leading our people, our native land, out of misery
    and suffering,
Let us join our efforts in the fight for the building of
    a new life.
Let us stand up and break our chains.
For too long have we swallowed our hatred.
Let us keep ready for all sacrifices and our life will
    be radiant.
Ceaselessly for the people's cause we struggle,
Hastening to the battlefield!
Forward! All together advancing!
Our Vietnam is strong eternal.

Van Cao later noted that he wanted to write a song that was understandable to all its listeners or singers. Ho Chi Minh thought so highly of the song that, five days before the founding of the DRV, he chose "Forward March" as the state's national anthem. This choice was confirmed by a government decree in the 1980s.

Like other artists in Vietnam, Van Cao discovered that his freedom of expression was limited to writing or painting subjects that presented the government in a favorable light. In the late 1950s, Van Cao, along with like-minded artists, began publishing *Nhan Van*. This journal criticized the government's handling of the land-redistribution program. It also accused the government of killing thousands of landlords.

For their criticism, more than forty of Van Cao's colleagues were imprisoned. Van Cao was not incarcerated, but he was told to stop writing and painting. For thirty years, he obeyed the government's orders. Following *doi moi*, however, Van Cao's songs were once again heard on government radio stations. His music was featured at more than sixty performances in 1987. During the last years of his life, Van Cao complained that his best creative years were wasted because of the government-imposed silence. Nevertheless, this artist remains one of Vietnam's most noted songwriters as well as the author of the country's national anthem.

Tran Tien

He does not like to be called a pop musician, but Tran Tien is one of Vietnam's most popular modern-day musicians. He was born in Ha Tay Province in 1947, and he came of age during the Second Indochina War. He was sent to the front during the war, and he served as a cultural cadre.

His popularity is due to his rich blending of Vietnamese folk songs with jazz, rock, and country elements from the West. Tran Tien insists that he does not listen to other musical artists, yet his songs are often compared to those of Western artists.

A distinctive element in Tran Tien's songs is that they often tell detailed stories. One of his most popular songs, "Older Sister," is an example of the narrative in his lyrics. This piece tells the story of a sister who foregoes marriage for the sake of her mother and her younger siblings. Tran Tien explained that there is usually one family member that sacrifices for the others. He wrote "Older Sister" for the Vietnamese who do without for the sake of relatives.

Tien has continued to make an impact on Vietnam's music scene through the promotion of his niece, Thu Ha. A graduate of Hanoi's Conservatory of Music, Thu Ha acknowledges that her musical influences include Western blues, gospel, rock, and jazz. She won Vietnam's top singer award in 1999, and her concert performances are sold out. Thu Ha often sings with her uncle and the performances are very reminiscent of the large concert events in the West.

Without the implementation of *doi moi,* it is probable that there would be continued restrictions on Vietnamese artists. Tran Tien and Van Cao are just two examples of artists who endured difficult times, and emerged full of creativity.

The Education System in Vietnam

It is appropriate that this book concludes with a description of Vietnam's education system. Scholarship has always been prized in this Southeast Asian society. Taking their cue from Confucian philosophy, Vietnamese emperors chose their advisors from the scholarly elite class. Beyond the earlier-noted rewards that Vietnamese gained by passing government tests, a Vietnamese scholar was considered a virtuous gentleman, which was the primary goal of Confucian adherents.

In 1976, the SRV restructured the country's education system. It began by closing all private schools. The country's Communist party wanted its youth to appreciate socialist values. Private schools, particularly those affiliated with Buddhist or Christian institutions, were beyond the control of the government, so they were ordered closed. However, because of the problems noted immediately below, private schools in Vietnam are once again thriving.

After years of experimentation, the SRV has established a four-tier education program for its citizens. All children between six and eleven years of age attend primary school. This encompasses grades one to five. After primary school, those students aspiring to higher education move on to lower secondary studies, or grades six through nine. Primary school graduates who do not evidence a propensity for scholarship are encouraged to attend a three-year vocational training program. Many who follow this path eventually work in service-oriented occupations.

Graduates of lower secondary studies move on to upper secondary schools, which encompasses grades ten through twelve. Twelfth-grade graduates take college entrance exams. Unfortunately, the higher education system is so strapped that only about one-third of university applicants are accepted. Students who cannot enter university training, either return to farming, or take the entrance exam the following year. Some private secondary schools claim that they can guarantee that their

Vietnamese children race towards the camera. One–third of Vietnam's population is under fifteen years of age, and sixty percent are under thirty.

graduates will pass the university entrance exams. Wealthy parents send their children to these prestigious prep schools.

While Vietnam boasts a highly literate population, it continues to face major challenges in its education system. First, there is a growing crisis of personnel. In the mid-1990s, the SRV reported that it faced a deficit of 60,000 elementary teachers. One reason for this is that half the country's population is under twenty years of age. There are many students to teach. For those who do teach, however, the financial compensation is appallingly low. In fact, those students who leave school for service-oriented jobs, generally earn more than four times that of school teachers. Most Vietnamese teachers must have night jobs to make ends meet.

Finally, Vietnam, which boasts a literacy rate of ninety-four percent, is failing in its attempt to educate many of its ethnic minority groups. Despite the government's policy to monetarily reward teachers who volunteer to teach in the highlands, there is a dearth of educators in these more remote regions of the country. Even where there are schools, most of the indigenous highlanders cannot afford to let their children, who help in the fields, attend classes.

Conclusion

For two thousand years, the Vietnamese have steadily carved out a society and culture that has faced numerous external pressures. But like the resilient bamboo plant, the Vietnamese have bent but never broken under their trials. At the start of the twenty-first century, Vietnam is in a somewhat unprecedented situation. It is at peace with its neighbors and with the world. Now, it must face its greatest challenge: itself.

The Communist leaders of this great country are trying to mend their nation by allowing greater economic and education freedoms. At the same time, they continue to prescribe the limits of liberty. These inconsistencies make domestic and foreign businesses wary of investing in Vietnam. In fact, the real difficulty Vietnam faces today is its desire to fit an ideology into a world that follows the beat of a different economic drum. The results of *doi moi* are mixed as the SRV government continues to keep a tight control on the country's education and economy.

After defeating the world's greatest powers, Vietnam's final war might be with itself.

INDEX

Page numbers in *italics* denote illustrations